Contents

GLAMOUR MAGICK FOR THE SOUL

SPELLS TO BE A BAD A$$ WITCH

JENNY TOUPIN

Gilded Grimoire Press

First Edition

ISBN: 9798989226009

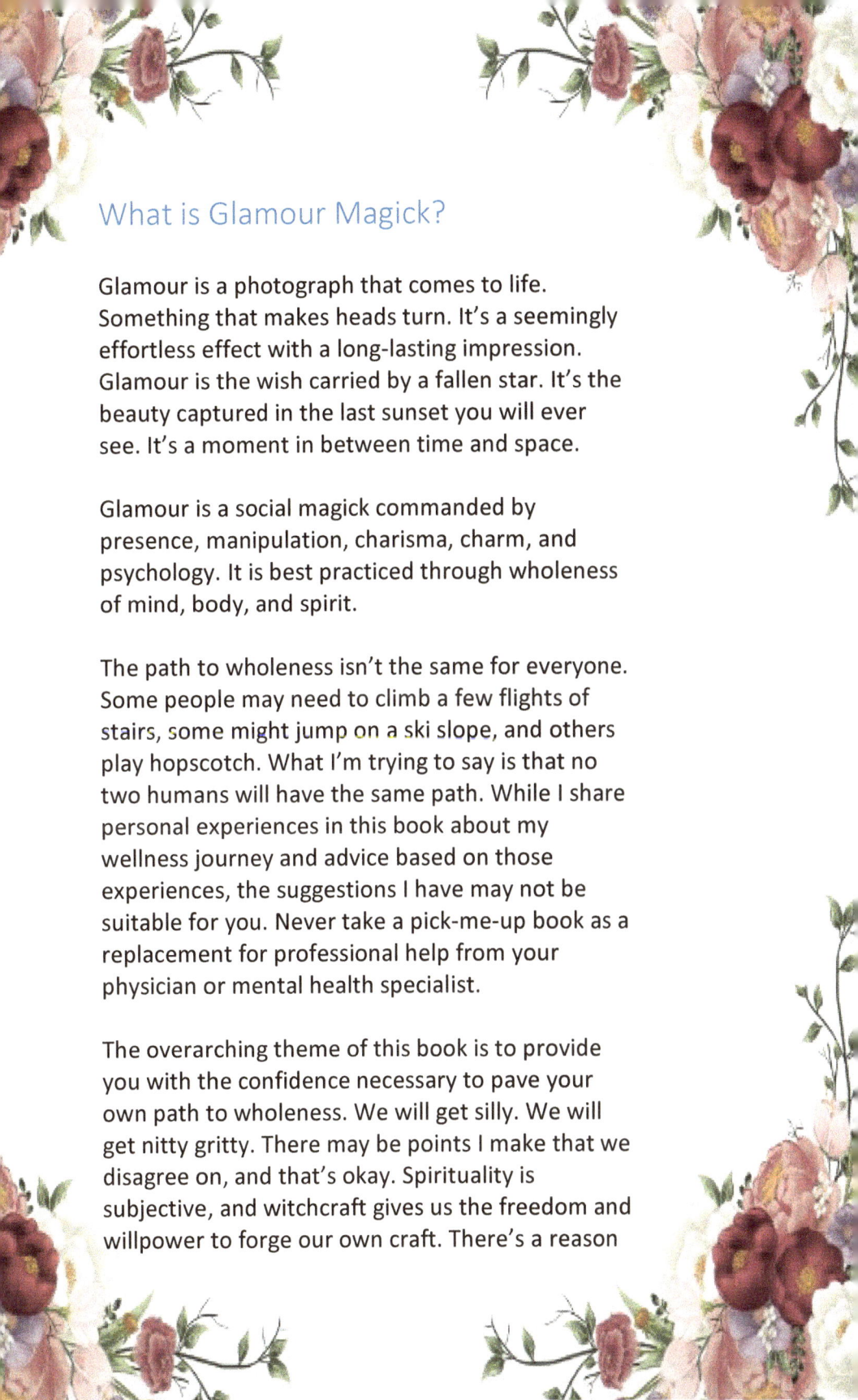

What is Glamour Magick?

Glamour is a photograph that comes to life. Something that makes heads turn. It's a seemingly effortless effect with a long-lasting impression. Glamour is the wish carried by a fallen star. It's the beauty captured in the last sunset you will ever see. It's a moment in between time and space.

Glamour is a social magick commanded by presence, manipulation, charisma, charm, and psychology. It is best practiced through wholeness of mind, body, and spirit.

The path to wholeness isn't the same for everyone. Some people may need to climb a few flights of stairs, some might jump on a ski slope, and others play hopscotch. What I'm trying to say is that no two humans will have the same path. While I share personal experiences in this book about my wellness journey and advice based on those experiences, the suggestions I have may not be suitable for you. Never take a pick-me-up book as a replacement for professional help from your physician or mental health specialist.

The overarching theme of this book is to provide you with the confidence necessary to pave your own path to wholeness. We will get silly. We will get nitty gritty. There may be points I make that we disagree on, and that's okay. Spirituality is subjective, and witchcraft gives us the freedom and willpower to forge our own craft. There's a reason we call it that, *the craft*. Your spiritual journey is an art, and the paintbrush is in your hands.

I had once asked a group of people what the first thing was that came to mind when hearing the term 'glamour magick.' My favorite response was an exchange between Marilyn Monroe and her photographer's wife, Amy Greene. My second favorite response was 'glitter.' Amy Greene had said:

"I'll never forget the day Marilyn and I were walking around New York City, just having a stroll on a nice day. She loved New York because no one bothered her there like they did in Hollywood, she could put on her plain-Jane clothes and no one would notice her. She loved that. So, as we were walking down Broadway, she turns to me and says, 'Do you want to see me become her?' I didn't know what she meant but I just said 'Yes' — and then I saw it. I don't know how to explain what she did because it was so very subtle, but she turned something on within herself that was almost like magic. And suddenly cars were slowing, and people were turning their heads and stopping to stare. They were recognizing that this was Marilyn Monroe as if she pulled off a mask or something, even though a second ago nobody noticed her. I had never seen anything like it before." (Edie Weinstein, The Marilyn Monroe Effect: The Nonverbal Communication of Confidence, 2019)

A common misconception about glamour is that it's all about the looks. Or rather, looks and luxury. But it's so much more than that. It's not only physical but also mental and spiritual. You can shift any type of energy through a glamour.

This magick has existed for a long time, but it looks much different today than what it used to be. It's more of an umbrella term now for anything involving self-care, beauty, and indulgence. Glamour has its roots in fae magick, specifically in stories of glamour being used to make the fae invisible. It didn't actually make them invisible, just out of sight to the human eye. Fae magick has a reputation for being mischievous and deceitful. These aren't always negative traits and most often just misunderstood. Whatever the case, there are practicalities for all types of magick. Glamour allows the witch to go unseen, much like how the fae used it for a thousand years.

In today's world, we use glamour magick for the opposite as well, to be social creatures. As with the upward trend in technology, communication has evolved. Social media has encouraged communication to be impersonal. Opting for always texting over calling your friends can erect social barriers and pose challenges for effective communication. Each generation loses some of those face-to-face personal connection skills.

Without that in-person interaction, glamour magick can be difficult. But like everyone else in the world, witches adapt. Mastering the allure of a glamour makes that in-person spell all the more potent. And those same energies can travel at a distance with the right focus.

We can easily command the attention of a room. We can create a presence of awe or even sadness. With glamour, we use our personal energy to shift and seep into the surrounding energies to enact change.

Using glamour gives the wielder a high on life. But please note that the user can easily overdo it, and this magick should not be used all the time. Eventually, overusing a glamour may lead to the opposite effect, making the user repulsive rather than alluring.

When we use glamour, most often the witch will want to create the effect of a charm or allure. We hold mystery in our eyes, and like hypnosis, we can draw certain energies to ourselves. Rather than standard ritual tools, we use things like aesthetics, aromatherapy, sound, and touch. We rely heavily on our senses and project them to those around us. By manipulating aesthetics, we create an environment that is synthetic.

Psychology is another major component of a glamour spell, one serving as a boost to our mental health that can project feelings and emotions onto other people. The most powerful forms of magick are the most subtle.

Physical attributes and presence play a big part in glamour. If you need the glamour to last awhile, it's best to imbue your magick into an object you can wear, like clothing, makeup, or jewelry. To do so, you just need a simple binding spell. Instead of ignoring red flags, here's your chance to wear them. Take control of your life. What one person may assess as a flaw could prove to be a merit to another.

Infusing Glamour in an Object

In the times we need a boost most, the day is usually already going poorly and hard to turn around. Because of this, I want to give you a spell that allows you to bottle up some glamour for later. The best part about these leftovers is that they don't expire. When you're having a good day and feeling more like yourself, try taking a bit of that good mood and bottling it up for later. In this spell, we are going to infuse that power into an object.

Pick something that makes you feel beautiful or just generally good about yourself. Bless or anoint it with your preferred essential oil and put it in the center of your altar during your next ritual. The specifics of the oil do not matter since we are not looking for a specific metaphysical attribute. Instead, pick one you already have or a scent that attracts you the most. If you don't have much experience working with oils, floral scents are lighter and if you like earthy scents, try patchouli or sandalwood.

Light a candle that represents your intent and carve a sacred symbol or word representing your desire at the base. These herbs and crystals are suggestions based on their metaphysical properties related to binding.

Feel free to add your own spin, but these are my recommendations: Use herbs like basil, bloodroot, elder berries/flowers, mandrake, and myrtle. Keep crystals around like labradorite, malachite, tiger's eye, and tourmaline. Even better, if you include any of these stones in your jewelry.

The words for the enchantment aren't as important as your intent and willpower. Here is my example, but I encourage you to always compose your own spells. Even if you just add a simple twist. They need your personality to cater to you. Chant over the object of binding.

Chant:

"I infuse my love, my light, my lust
For later use on terms I trust

To douse myself in confidence
Allure and riddle in my nature
Command attention—dominance
Like sirens inducing sailors

May my eyes pierce through the soul
May no lies break through my hold
May my voice command respect
My touch, a rousing effect

My requests will be demands
With servants at my hand
Like Medusa and her serpent gaze

I'll leave them in a dreary haze"

Those who adhere to the law of attraction and the concept of glamour magick share similarities.

The concept of glamour magick is steeped in the belief that thoughts translate into energy. The law of attraction illustrates that negative thoughts generate negative experiences, while positive thinking generates positive outcomes. It's a belief that those strong thoughts translate into energy, which is the same way we use glamour.

"Thoughts become things. If you can see it in your mind, you can hold it in your hand." (Proctor)

While the law of attraction is a decent concept, be wary of toxic positivity. Never suppress your negative emotions and bottle them up. I just want you to try acknowledging your positives more often, because we tend to manifest what we think about more often.

So, if you think of yourself as glamourous, baby, you *are* glamourous. But you don't need to put up a front on days you really aren't feeling it. Everyone is allowed to have bad days.

Since in magick, our tools and methods revolve around symbolism, magnets are a common ritual tool to attract things to you.

My favorite stone is hematite. Hematite has many purposes, such as grounding, absorbing your negative energy and, of course, attraction. Please note that not all hematite has magnetic properties; its composition varies. Most magnetic hematite is not hematite at all, but a manufactured ceramic look-alike with iron. Though they still hold the same metaphysical properties. Here's the simplest spell to manifest your desires with the law of attraction.

Supplies:
2 pieces of hematite
Small strip of paper
Pen/pencil

Instruction:
Write your desire on the small strip of paper. It should be the size of a fortune cookie slip. Don't use card stock or anything too thick, otherwise the spell won't work. After you've written your desire, fold the sheet of paper in half just once. Then take the two pieces of hematite and lock them together, sandwiching the paper in the middle.

Chant:

"As I wish it
It will be
I will get
What I decree

I decree that _____ will come to me"

Fill in the blank with your desire. This could be money, love, a friend, inspiration, or anything. After you speak your desires into existence, leave the hematite and note on your altar or somewhere you will see it often.

When combating writer's block, I leave it on my desk next to my PC. This way, as I'm staring deeply at the flashing vertical line in Microsoft Word, my peripherals always have eyes on my desires. And inspiration always comes to me shortly after.

The law of attraction isn't something of coincidence or circumstance. In order to achieve your goals, you must work toward them. Magick is the first step but by far isn't the last. You're not going to meet people sitting at home in a book. You're not going to get a new job if you don't apply for one. And so forth.

Glamour also manifests through the power of suggestion. Émile Coué in his book, *Self-Mastery Through Conscious Autosuggestion,* (1922) discusses tendencies in our unconscious self versus our conscious self, as well as how our will affects our ability to execute tasks. This bears resemblance to the practice of hypnotism. Here are four laws

Émile came up with after experiments regarding suggestion:

1. "When the will and the imagination are antagonistic, it is always the imagination which wins, without any exception.
2. In the conflict between the will and the imagination, the force of the imagination is in direct ratio to the square of the will.
3. When the will and the imagination are in agreement, one does not add to the other, but one is multiplied by the other.
4. The imagination can be directed. (The expressions "In direct ratio to the square of the will" and "Is multiplied by" are not rigorously exact. They are simply illustrations destined to make my meaning clearer.)"

(Coué, 1922)

Émile, in essence, is trying to say that we are our own worst critics. If we think we will fail at a task, we will. All the 'What Ifs' in our imagination will manifest if we expect negative impacts. If you are confident that you will succeed and manifest positivity, you are more likely to do so.

Whenever you have a day that seems like everything that could go wrong does, this is likely because of these laws. That one negative emotion is magnified. And even the smallest of hiccups in your day can make it seem like the world is crashing down.

Émile goes on to explain how this power of suggestion can even treat physical ailments. The suggestions put the body on course to naturally mend itself. Commands that trigger responses in your nervous system that are sent to the brain. A man with paralysis suddenly could walk again. Was it a miracle, or the true power of glamour?

These suggestions can be self-prescribed, or you can try them out on a friend or foe. Let's try a spell that involves suggestion. Pick a partner that doesn't share your same beliefs to give you some skepticism. Say you're going to help them meditate. (That's not a lie.)

The Art of Suggestion

Supplies:
A couch
A friend
A margarita

Instruction: The 'suggestion' below replaces our normal chant in this spell. Think of this like a guided meditation. Your voice will fade into the background of their subconscious, and the goal is to get this person to take your suggestion.

For whatever suggestion you are practicing, make sure you have a consenting partner. If you don't have one, you can practice on yourself. Make your intentions clear so that they manifest. You also don't want to lie and call yourself a professional hypnotist. We're not playing psychology, and it's important to be respectful to mental health professionals. We are merely using the influence of hypnotism and suggestion as a tool to better our craft.

Smoking will serve as the common subject for hypnotism in this example. In this scenario, your partner wants to quit smoking but is having difficulty. Your partner **must** be willing for this to work effectively. Otherwise, they wouldn't have agreed to lie on your couch and let you try this experiment.

In this spell, we are suggesting cigarettes are harmful to your body. The suggestion is that they are painful, and through working in the subconscious, hopefully they will no longer be desirable in the conscious self. Make your partner fully aware that this is the intent and be sure they are still onboard.

Once the key points for the suggestion have been met, have them lay down, relax, shut their eyes, and practice proper breathing techniques. Have them count down from ten, one number per exhale. You need them to focus on just breathing and existing. You don't want their thoughts to roam. Oh, and the margarita is for you and your victory drink.

<u>Suggestion</u>:

"I'm going to count back from ten. At each number, you will exhale. When I reach one, you will be in a trance. You are relaxed. You are safe.

It's the end of the day. You are exhausted. You had a hard day. You're tired. You reach for your cigarettes.

You put your hand in your pocket and your hand feels numb. You have the feeling of sharp needles crawling up your arm. It's painful.

You remove a cigarette from the pack. The filter burns your fingers. You drop it on the ground. You're on fire. You're burning. You run to get some water and wash the burn.

You feel better. You go back to grab another cigarette. Again, the numbness returns. You take the cigarette from the pack. It doesn't burn to the touch.

You put it to your lips. It's burned your mouth. The skin from your lips is melting off. The pain is so drastic, you cry out and again rush for some water. You feel better.

You take the rest of the cigarettes and throw the pack into the toilet. You flush them. They no longer serve your purpose. They don't comfort you. You don't need them. I am going to count back from ten. After each number, you will exhale. When I reach one, you will be awake."

In this example of auto-suggestion, notice my short and choppy sentences. You want to be abrupt, but you don't want to babble. You're not telling a horror story; you are helping someone meditate through suggestion. Please note that this doesn't work on all types of people.

This also works when someone is asleep. (Please be sure they're actually asleep.) You can chant suggestions to someone who is in REM or dreaming. If you are worried they will wake up, you can make these suggestions in your head with a focus on the person.

Glamour is quite simple and doesn't need any intricacies to work. A common practice among those who include glamour in the craft is color coordination. Colors set moods and help us imagine certain elements and feelings within our mind's eye.

Color Coordination in Glamour

You probably already use color coordination with candles and crystals. In glamour, we extend the magick to any aesthetic you can imagine. Our clothes and makeup are a huge part of how we immerse ourselves into our glamour.

Wear black to ground yourself and create a powerful presence. Black is heavy. It's a color of change and shadow work. It's also naturally slimming and offers an edge. When you wear black, you manifest control and attention.

Wear white to feel as light as the wind. When you crave freedom and free-form, white is the color for you. Wear it to seek enlightenment and to put those around you at ease.

Wear red to inspire awe. Use it to attract lust and passion. Be aggressive with your spellwork and show your strength when using this color. Red is love. Red is anger. Red is raw.

Wear orange to be *loud*. Orange overflows with happiness and freshness. It will make you feel bold.

Wear yellow to form strong bonds. Feel summer in every footstep. Use it to brighten someone's day and make smiles become contagious.

Wear green to attract abundance in your life. Whether that abundance is in the form of wealth or options, green will rope in these desires. Silvers and golds pair well with green.

Wear blue to overcome sadness. When you are overwhelmed and choking on your feelings, blue will wash away the pain. This color will catch your tears and turn them into a well that cleanses you.

Wear purple to awaken your third eye. To feel more spiritually connected to your higher self or the divine. Purple is the color of dreams and prophecy. If you want your intuition to speak loudly, this is the color you want to wear.

It's all about *aesthetic*.

Sensory perception is key to practicing glamour magick. It's about touch, taste, sight, sounds, scents, and feelings. Describing these perceptions pertaining to art is called **aesthetic**.

In glamour, *you* are an aesthetic. You are the art. But like all art, it is subjective to the eyes of the beholder. An aesthetic is felt differently depending on the person. The utilization of aesthetics to your advantage requires a significant amount of sociological studies.

What is beauty to you? Is it the bleeding sky of a summer sunset? Is it hushed words whispered from bright red lips? Take note of things you find to be beautiful. What happens in the presence of these places, people, and things? Do your pupils dilate? Do you tremble? Does your heart skip a beat?

After you know your definition of beauty, perhaps try looking at things from a cultural standpoint. What were the beauty standards drilled into your head as a teenager? Was it the fierceness of a CoverGirl model judged by Tyra Banks? Was it that popular girl in high school with bleach-blonde hair, big breasts, and Hollister clothing?

But like yourself, others may not fall in line with cultural definitions of modern beauty standards. To have an effective glamour, you need to study your target before curating your aesthetic.

Try different things and gauge reactions. Note body language, tone of voice, and if their eyes match their smile. While high ritual for glamour can be fun and rewarding, a lot of this magick is done in the moment or on a whim. You need a sharp tongue, piercing eyes, and assertive body language no matter what type of glamour you're trying to achieve.

Denis Dutton came up with six universal truths of the power of aesthetics.

1.   Expertise or virtuosity.
2.   Non-utilitarian pleasure.
3.   Style.
4.   Criticism.
5.   Imitation.
6.   Special focus.
(Dutton, 2002)

Regarding expertise and virtuosity, everyone has an aesthetic. Certain characteristics and skills are admired as art.

Practice makes perfect. You can be naturally persuasive, or you could simply study persuasion and adapt your techniques over time. No artist makes their masterpiece the first time they pick up a paintbrush. Even if you are born with a gift, a skill is earned. While everyone might have an aesthetic, not everyone knows how to use it to their advantage. That's where glamour comes in.

Non-utilitarian pleasure refers to greater purpose rather than practicalities. The aesthetic is the pleasure, and the experience achieved through art. This is the effect you want to have on people. If you look at a painting and don't feel it, then either you aren't the target audience, or the artist failed to convey their purpose to you. If you are reading a fiction novel and can't grasp a connection to the characters, you aren't fully taking in the experience. With all witchcraft, there is always a purpose. The experience is the manifestation of that glamour, what you project into your environment and others around you. Whether you want to make someone sweat, their heartbeat escalate, or scream. That power is in your hands as the artist to craft the experience.

Style is unique to the person. Though you can mimic an aesthetic, you must find your own style to make it work. Otherwise, you won't stand out in a crowd. Having style is being able to take something that already exists and make it special.

Be unique. Remember in Mean Girls when Regina George was sabotaged and had holes cut in her shirt around her breasts? She was confident instead of embarrassed and wore her outfit proudly, and the next day everyone in the school was mimicking her style. So, style isn't always being the most 'attractive.' It's instead being different and visually loud.

Accept criticism with grace. Instead of discounting advice or criticism, truly listen to people that show interest. An ugly trait is someone who takes criticism defensively. But if the person giving you advice isn't your target of glamour, remember that it is subjective. To each their own. You will never be able to please everyone.

Imitation is a compliment and adds to your aesthetic. Now, this doesn't mean someone should infringe on copyright or take credit where it's not deserved. Though, someone following in your footsteps isn't always a bad thing. Successful glamours grab attention. People will see what you're doing and see that it works. In turn, they will want to reap your success through imitation.

Special focus refers to exactly that: focus. As was stated earlier, you can't please everyone. Deal with a single niche and be great at it. Focus on one person. One object. Give all your alertness to one project at a time and make it great. Having a clear focus will help you manifest your glamour more quickly and effectively.

Like colors and aesthetics, the elements could also be used to strengthen your glamour spells. (Earth, Air, Water and Fire) Somewhere along your magick path and studies, you've likely stumbled upon these elements and how they correlate to magick and ritual. You have your quarters, watchtowers, or elements; however, you want to refer to them. And before any spell, you cast a circle by evoking these elements. I used to do this before I realized formalities weren't always necessary to practice magick.

Elemental Glamours

Despite what is mentioned above, it is still a good basis for your magick practice and frankly a good idea to build a relationship with the earth and the elemental forces that guide us. Even if you don't cast circles within your personal practice, I still suggest building these relationships and evoking elementals when it makes sense with your intent.

You can say these elements by name: Air, Fire, Water, Earth. Alternatively, you can give them a name or associate them with a related deity. I don't mention spirit here simply because every spell you do should include this. In every glamour, you should call to your heart, your soul, and your spirit. This is a trinity that will guide not only your magick, but also your way of life. Let your heart lead to your passions. Your soul is the life force that drives you, while spirit awakens you to deeper connections with the divine.

For air magick, I work with Aether. This is the element I have an affinity with that I feel closest to. The more you work with the elements, the more you will realize which one resonates with you most.

When you evoke them, your candle flame will always be brighter. The chills up your spine will be more intense. And with air, when I summon him, he always responds with a gust of friendly wind. Call to air in your glamours when your intent is creativity and transformation. With glamours being so closely tied to art, you will call to air often. And of course, with transformation, that comes in every glamour. You are either manifesting qualities you do not normally possess, or you are enhancing existing qualities.

For fire magick, I work with Logi. Fire is used in any magick to incite love, lust, passion, and aggression. From friendships to sailed ships, fire is a friend you want in your corner. The most popular glamours are those used for seduction. You want to look, feel, and possess fire whenever this is your intent.

For water magick, I work with Aegir. In any magick, water is the element of healing, cleansing, and fulfillment. In glamour, we use water to heal ourselves from harmful self-talk and to boost our confidence. We use ritual baths to cleanse ourselves and to wash off our glamours, or to prepare for a new one. Water is also important in scrying when we use mirror magick.

For earth magick, I work with Gaia. Traditionally, you work with earth for grounding. This is especially helpful when we later discuss how to mask our energies or when you've had enough of glamour and want to turn it off. Work with earth through meditation and your root chakra, also referred to as your kundalini energy. Kundalini is associated with the snake, the concept that the structure of your spine holds the energy of a serpent spirit. In mythology, we recognize the serpent correlates to sexual energy and shadow work. You may be familiar with the Aesclepius wand shown below. It is an emblem dedicated to the Greek god of healing and is a serpent coiled around a stave. This makes working with earth spirits and deities critical to using most glamour magick.

(Unknown, Asclepius, Greco-Roman marble statue)

Glamour is about stepping outside of your comfort zone. It's being thwarted into the most bizarre role and winning the Grammy. Change up the ways you do your makeup. Wear items that make you bold and stand out from others. Confidence isn't quiet.

Makeup is an easy item to infuse your glamour into. The beauty world for cosmetics has been a rough crowd for many years. The people that live in the industry often find themselves in cutthroat situations. As someone who just uses the product, you don't have to involve yourself in that. Don't pick styles and products because of who made them; pick the mediums you want to use to build upon yourself. Drugstore makeup or leftovers from a friend's haul is fine. No judgement here. Treat your makeup selections much like choosing a new crystal. Pick it up and do an energy check. Make sure you're on the same frequency.

Makeup is no longer gatekept by a specific identity or gender. We have queens in the industry who were bold enough to show us we all have the right to beauty. But makeup and clothing choices aren't the only way we can use glamour.

Even the way you move can affect your glamour. Your walk, your body language, and your eye contact are all important in setting your illusion. When you walk slowly, more people stare. It's just like when you whisper, more people will try to listen.

Calculate your hand movements like they contribute to the meaning of your words. Put emphasis on maintaining eye contact when you tilt your head or swipe your hair behind your ear. Putting your hair behind your ear is a psychological tactic to show others you are listening. Hand gestures can place attention back on you when you're trying to explain something.

Look at someone like they're the only person in the room. Don't look at them like you understand them, but rather like you are looking through them. Like you *are* them.

When you smile, look down and back up at someone. Flash it quickly as a treat, like it was caused by something someone else did. Make them want more.

When you speak, wait a moment after you part your lips. Let your breath linger and disperse your energy like a cloud of psychic smoke. Make sure someone listens.

Speak only with purpose and leave out filler. Small talk, quick speech, loud abruptness, and sharp tongues can make people nervous and sit on the edge of their seat. And that's great if that's your intention. Though, if you want to entice someone, speak softly and slowly. Speak as if you're serenading someone into revealing their deepest, darkest secrets.

All of this you likely already do unintentionally. As a witch who is used to reading energies and playing on empathy, you are likely sensitive to how simple things like tone and body language affect people.

Like Marilyn Monroe, this is how you turn 'on' your glamour.

Turning on your glamour will heighten your senses and help you read those around you who may be too difficult at first glance. This also helps when you need to interact with a stranger, or in general with breaking the ice. We can push our energy onto others all day, but if you can't read the other person, it may not work. You can't and shouldn't change something you cannot understand.

So, I'm going to teach you how to be a little more empathetic. You won't truly understand other's intentions or energies on your first try. To do this requires practice and patience. My biggest tip is to not get overwhelmed and use this ability too much. That's my 'be careful what you wish for' advice. Use this tool to help understand people, not to take on their burdens and grocery list of issues.

It can get addicting to read people. Believe me, I've been there. And you can easily lose yourself in the process. Glamour illusion. So theoretically, you should be able to break that illusion at any time. If you find you can't, you've gone too far.

That's with any spell, not just this one. Meditate before trying this spell and be sure you understand your own aura and emotional state first. Here's a spell to turn on your empathy and effectively, turn on your glamour.

Clap On

Supplies:
Aura quartz (clear quartz)
Water dish

Instruction:
Eventually, you will be able to turn on glamour without the help. It will simply be muscle memory. But to get you started, take an aura quartz and a dish of water. Bless the quartz as you say the following chant, lightly blessing it with water from the dish. Afterward, place the quartz in a windowsill or outside on your property so it can refract light. The sun charges it. Carry the crystal with you and hold it in your palm when you want to activate the glamour.

Chant:

"May those who meet my gaze
Be enamored by my blaze

Thus, their auras will shine bright
So, I can read their ebbing light"

Remember How to Love Yourself

A great deal of witchcraft is self-care. There is magic in realizing your worth, your beauty, and your strength. Self-care isn't selfish. In this book, I will teach you how to sync your spirituality with your heart. A lot of these tips you may be already doing, not even realizing how they can be connected to your magick and craft work.

The first step in learning to love yourself again is re-surfacing the traumas that made you feel undeserving. No matter how much you think you deserve punishment or bad karma, you are entitled to kindness. You *deserve* happiness.

Think about all the people in your life. Make a list of how you remember helping them, happy memories, and how they help you. Then make another list of the opposite and how those people have negatively affected you. Ultimately, it is your choice on whether to keep people in your life who have hurt you. For each negative, you need to decide on if that action is forgivable. Even if one is not and everything else can be resolved, you can't let it slip. If you can't forgive, you can't choose to live in hurt.

Your first option is to then confront this person about how they hurt you and how their actions affect you. If that doesn't relieve the hurt or if you cannot muster the courage to speak to the person on the matter, it's not fair to either of you to keep them in your circle. It's not fair for you to live in constant hurt by this trauma in the back of your head, and it's not fair to them to be constantly resented with the false pretense that they have been forgiven.

You can still love someone and let them go. The hardest decision you will ever make is letting go of love that still has its flame. However, if the flame struggles and flickers, it's time to put it out. If in the future you are in good shape to try to re-kindle that flame, then perhaps things can be given another try.

For now, however, it's time to free yourself. The best way to do that with someone you've had a strong connection with is through a cord cutting ceremony. This is best done including the personal effects of each party.

Cord Cutting

Supplies:
2 candles
Tool to carve on the wax
Twine
Personal effects of the person you wish to cut ties with
Optional: Oils and herbs that you feel represent you and the person

Instruction:
You will need two candles, one to represent yourself and one to represent the person you want to cut ties with. I prefer to use candles in the shape of a person and to carve names at the base of them. You'll end up putting the candles parallel to each other and wrapping the string around the candles several times and tying a knot.

Keep the personal effects close to each respective candle, but not close enough that there is a risk of catching fire. Personal items could be a picture, a trinket, or even hair from a brush. Preferably, make it symbolic of your relationship with this person. It is optional to dress the candles, but I like to dab them with essential oil. To represent myself, I use rose oil, as it's my preferred scent. I had a partner that always wore earthy scents like sandalwood and patchouli, so I would dress items dedicated to him with those oils.

You can say a spell or mantra to intensify this spell, but it's truly all about your personal willpower. If your desire to have this person in your life outweighs your own mental health, it won't work.

When you light the candles, don't imagine any ill intent toward this person. Just keep your strength and remind yourself that you are deserving of truth. You deserve happiness. You deserve love. This person cannot control your feelings. You are in charge of your response.

Eventually, the candles will burn down and if effective, the string will burn as well, literally severing the knot you had with this person.

Take a deep breath. You did it. Be proud of yourself. *You let go*. You are ready for love and light.

Now that you have made room in your heart for yourself, it's time to pamper. When was the last time you've bought something nice for yourself? Here are some ideas to treat yourself:

- Go get your favorite coffee
- Get a haircut
- Have your nails done
- Buy a new outfit
- Indulge in a new book

Maybe money is tight. That's okay. Giving yourself time is just as important. Take time to finish that book that's been on your nightstand for five months. Turn off the TV and go outside to listen to the birds sing. Instead of a shower, take a nice long bath. We'll talk about ritual baths in the next section, *Creating a Safe Space.*

Remember: **Those Who Hurt Us Don't Deserve Us**.

If you lack self-confidence, chances are you don't like to look at yourself in the mirror. You don't want to see yourself naked. And you most certainly can't accept a compliment.

The next step in learning to love ourselves is working positive affirmations into a mantra. Make a list catered to your insecurities and re-write it in a way that pivots them into positivity.

Let's say, for example, that you think you are physically unattractive. This is the label you have given yourself. For the first part of the mantra, write down that you are beautiful. For another example, let's say you feel you're on the verge of a breakdown on the daily. There's just too much to keep up with and not enough time. Add to the list that you are strong and that you are patient. Lastly, let's say you have a weight problem. Write down that you will make healthy choices today.

Now take your list first thing when you wake up and look in the mirror.

You may feel silly, but trust me, it works.

You are having a conversation with your spirit and your intent is to manifest. Even if you don't believe in what you wrote. Perhaps you don't feel beautiful, or you don't trust yourself to make good choices. The point is, we are re-routing your way of thinking to fuel your willpower, your spirit and your well from which you pull your magick from.

Maintain eye contact with yourself. Your mantra should sound something like this:

I am beautiful.
I am strong.
I am patient.
I will make healthy choices today.

Your task is to repeat this daily in the mirror until you believe it and these traits are manifested. Reclaim your name. Don't let others tell you who you are. Reclaim your pain. Take control of your trauma.

On your glamourous journey, I want you to try keeping a journal to log your progress. Break it up into sections every day. All you need is two: **This is What Sucked Today**, and **This is What Was Great Today**. Log every day. If you see a pattern of what was negative being constant and unchanging, you need to take action.

After you've had the repetition of writing your daily quirks, I want you to solve one negative problem each day and find a way to make it positive. So, the next day, you get to write about another great thing. I'll give an example below of what your journal entry might look like. Then we'll analyze how to make the next day 1% more bearable.

This is What Sucked Today	This is What Was Great Today
I'm overwhelmed at work	I had a good night with my partner
I didn't lose weight this week	My daughter scored a goal in soccer
My dog destroyed my favorite book	

While the above isn't actually my day today, those are very real things that happen. I need to look into myself and see the good in the things that bring me down. Let's reframe. We'll start out with work.

Everyone gets overwhelmed at work. It wouldn't be work if it was easy. I am overwhelmed at the moment, but I know it will eventually ease up and I can push through this. So instead of letting work drain me, I need to reframe and turn this into a positive. So tomorrow, my positive will be something like this:

My boss gives me more work because she trusts my work ethic and me. I can take my skills and strive for continuous improvement to increase my wealth and satisfaction in myself.

Or this:
I have struggled with weight for a long time. I've always been overweight and struggled with eating disorders. I'm not losing weight despite being in a caloric deficit, and I'm not getting the quick results

41

I want. However, I am making healthier choices. I am part of a rigorous exercise program in which I'm building muscle and strength. I realize muscle weighs more than fat. I am getting stronger and healthier, and I don't need to starve myself to do so.

So instead of being down about the slow-paced results of my weight loss, I need to reframe. Tomorrow, my positive will be something like this:

I am making healthier choices each day. I feel strong and have much more energy since I've been working out.

Lastly, we move onto my dog, Echo. She's a great dog and is an angel as long as someone is home. However, when she's alone, she has a naughty side and eats and destroys anything in sight. It's exhausting having to clean up an hour of mess after a full day at work and spend money to replace things, some of which is sentimental and not replaceable. To reframe this negative thought, I need to let go of my material attachment. At the end of the day, I love my pet. She is my companion and more important than any material item I own. Tomorrow, my positive will be something like this:

I am fortunate to have Echo as my companion. She is loving and provides comfort whenever I need it.

That's all it takes to reframe. It's up to you now to pinpoint your own issues and solutions. Note how framing doesn't solve problems per se, it merely solves your perception. Perception is key to having glamour in your life.

What is your identity? This isn't a simple question, and there shouldn't be a simple answer for anyone. Glamour can strengthen how you identify or the polar effect of transforming into another identity. We all have a nature and demeanor at any given time, and those two concepts don't always match up.

Nature is who you are on the inside. These are your traits that you couldn't change even if you tried. If you are an empathetic, gentle-loving creature, you can glamour yourself to be mean and apathetic, but glamour fades. You can't change your nature. It's part of your identity.

Demeanor is the show you put on for how you want others to perceive you. This isn't always intentional, but it can be. How I dress, how I act, how I speak, and my mannerisms are all a reflection of my demeanor.

For example, I was an alternative kid growing up. The names are always changing, but at the time, I was the emo girl, the scene kid, the creepy witch girl, the anime geek. Many people thought the way I dressed and acted was strange. *That's exactly what I wanted.*

I wanted to attract people that were like me. For my personal preference on beauty, I preferred cat eyes, black nail polish, plaid mini-skirts, Tripp pants, neon bows, and multi-colored wristbands, and leg warmers. I cosplayed and wore cat ears and cat tails and spoke weeb. Either this is foreign to you, or you get it. For the people that get it, you're the type of people I was trying to attract. People that I could be one-hundred percent myself around.

So, in short, create a demeanor that helps you identify with like-minded people. Your glamour is whatever makes you feel beautiful and comfortable. When you surround yourself with more of that energy, your glamour strengthens. There is power in numbers.

Re-framing into positive thinking can be utilized to target your unconscious thoughts as well. This is often called shadow work. Witchcraft adopted the phrase, originally coined by Carl Jung. The goal of shadow work is to target your unconscious mind to dig up what you repress.

When we lash out for something we deem silly later, it's often our repressed memories to blame. Shadow work not only improves the relationship with yourself but also your relationships with others. Recognizing that humanity isn't perfect and accepting our faults and flaws is embracing your shadow.

"A man who is possessed by his shadow is always standing in his own light and falling into his own traps. Whenever possible, he prefers to make an unfavorable impression on others." (Jung, 1953)

This is such a powerful quote. We are our own worst enemies. We have pathways for greatness but choose less because we feel that's what we deserve or what's comfortable. Without confidence, we portray ourselves as the low-life we see ourselves as. *That* is shadow. Shadow stops us from enlightenment and reaching the top of the pyramid of our hierarchy of needs. Dealing with our shadow will help make the impossible quite possible. Once you master and accept your shadow, you unlock power.

There can be no doubt that shadow stretches us out thinly sometimes. You need to acknowledge your past to move forward. In order to tap into your past, you need to figure out how the past affects your present. We develop unconscious behaviors to cope with situations that remind us of our past. But you may not realize that's what your mind is doing.

For example, let's say you had a partner that broke your trust and lied to you about having relations with someone else. You end that relationship and move on. Or do you? We've all felt cheated by a partner at one point in our lives. You likely carry trust issues over to present and future relationships because of this trauma.

This doesn't mean you can turn the effects of trauma off like a light switch. No. If it were that easy, we'd all do it. Getting to know your shadow self takes time, and it can't be rushed. Just simply be aware of your responses and how they affect you and those around you.

Maybe you spy on your partner's social media. You question where they are constantly. This is a reaction to your shadow. Once you identify your shadow, you can start healing and applying trust again. If you don't confront the reasons behind your negative behavior, it will cause the people around you to also exhibit poor behaviors. They may take your actions as possessiveness and the precursor to an abusive relationship, because you are deflecting your shadow.

Fight your fears. Shine a light on your shadow. Neither can exist without each other.

Shadow work puts emphasis on taking off the mask. But in glamour, we reclaim it. Go beyond your comfort zone. Shadow comes in the form of many things including selfishness, fear, anger, and greed. We can re-frame that shadow into self-care, a sense of wonder, passion, and achieving our goals.

Like anything else in glamour, we can manipulate our shadow to manifest our desires. No one is inherently bad, and no one is inherently good. We all come to this world with balance, and our environment and experiences can shift. It's our job to work with the shadow to get back into balance. We need glamour to heighten ourselves on a spiritual, physical, and emotional level.

I want you to go from a state of self-reflection to changing your reflection. Be the person you want to be. Be the person you are proud to look at in the mirror and can muster up a smile for. Chances are that this person is already inside you and it's time to bring them to the surface. Why are you limiting yourself?

While many of us are so focused on fixing our shadow self and accepting our traumas of the past, we often forget to take a deeper look at our personal light. Does your light align with your ethics and values, or do you follow society's perception of how you should think, act, and feel? Are your priorities in order?

To be successful with glamour magick, you must acknowledge that your light needs just as much work as your shadow. And when you grow as a person, they both grow together with you. You can start by defining your quirks and qualities, then evaluating them against your shadow and light. Once you do this, you can put on your mask. You're ready for glamour.

Balance Spell

Here is a ritual to maintain balance in your life between your shadow and light. The premise is simple. All you need to do is find a quiet place.

Supplies:
Only yourself!

Instruction:
Start by meditating through simple breathing techniques, standing in an upright position. If you are fortunate enough to have the option, be out in nature during this ritual. Close your eyes and leave your palms facing outward.

Continuing your breathing techniques, imagine a ball of white and yellow light forming in your right palm and a ball of darkness in your left hand. Try to image them at the same size, getting larger with each breath in, and slightly smaller with each breath out.

Chant:

"I accept my light
I accept the night

For in darkness, we have solace
In light, we have abundance
And in balance we have all of it"

Still keeping focus on the balls of light and darkness and your breathing, slowly raise your arms above your head. You should feel your heartrate decreasing. Tighten the muscles in your hands the closer you bring your palms together. You should feel a magnetic polarity pushing the forces apart. And when you finally clasp your hands together, release and feed the energy to your heart chakra.

A great hindrance to our ability to love ourselves is time. We become stressed over things we have no control over, and our work/life balances crash into shambles. We are drained spiritually, emotionally, mentally, and physically over this imbalance. This phenomenon is called burnout.

Things you love start to look like a chore. You lose your motivation. And your perception of the future becomes cynical.

While burnout can be caused by a number of events in your life, it's most commonly discussed in a work setting. Corporate America has a way of draining the life from you if you let it.

Here are some things to consider if you feel you are experiencing burnout:

- Are you getting enough sleep?
- What are your eating habits, including what you eat and when you eat?
- Have you tried writing a list of priorities?
- Do you think your work is meaningful?

Sleep is important for everyone's lives, not just us witches. If you are not getting enough sleep, you are not starting your day with full energy. Lacking a proper sleep schedule can cause fatigue, exacerbate depression and anxiety, and worsen irritability.

If you don't track what you eat, you should. It might surprise you what you put in your body daily. Even if you don't struggle with food, you should still track and maintain healthy habits. And you should reward yourself for maintaining a healthy lifestyle. Give praise.

In my experience, restrictive diets lead to unhealthy habits, so I avoid them. They work for many people; I'm just not one of them. If you struggle with food, try counting macros. This is good for anyone looking to lose weight or maintain/build muscle. And if you count macros, you'll notice you're eating a lot more than you're probably used to. Macro counts are different for everyone, so consult a nutritionist on what is healthy for you.

If the world is crashing down on you and you feel you don't have the time to get everything done, it's time to prioritize. You can manage your days digitally through your email calendar or traditionally through a planner or notebook. There's no reason you need to accomplish everything in one day. By looking at a larger scope spanned over a week's time, this will provide relief.

Plan accordingly and prioritize things that are urgent. You shouldn't task yourself with more than one urgent personal issue a day. Work can be another story. You may have several hot issues. They still all have a level of importance. Delegate if you can in the work setting.

When you are making your list of tasks and stressors, cross out anything that you don't have control over. That means anything you can't change. The most useful thing I learned from taking a stress management course in college was to not stress over things you can't control. This means other people's actions. You can be upset with your mom, your girlfriend, or your boss, but ultimately, you can't control their actions.

You can, however, influence them through spells and magick. And that's one way to take control. But remember that when you are doing this, you are also assuming responsibility for their actions. Before you glamour anyone else, really think about the implications of what you're doing. Is it worth it?

Before you take on others, you must first make sure all of your personal needs are met and that you aren't experiencing troubles with negative self-talk, your shadow, trauma, or burnout. This goes for helping others, as well. Make yourself the number one priority.

If someone effed you over, by all means, mess stuff up. If you have a friend in dire need of help, go for it. Just get your ducks in a row first. It's okay to believe in karma; I do. But I'm wise enough by now to know that sometimes karma takes too damn long. And 'black' magick isn't necessarily 'bad' magick. That's why we have deities that specialize in justice. Sometimes the universe needs to intervene.

And lastly, does your job provide you with satisfaction? If the answer is no, you need to look at your finances and evaluate whether you should start looking elsewhere. Your time is money. If you don't feel like your time is well spent, you have the power to change that.

Society these days puts guilt on people for taking time for themselves. It's the end of the world if you take a day off work when you're sick. Why buy yourself a pair of shoes when you have a perfectly good pair with holes in them? You shouldn't be watching TV; you should be cleaning until you can eat off of your floors. You get the picture.

We've all been in a scenario where we feel guilty for treating ourselves to simple, basic things. We strive to be perfect and skinny; a woman may have a breakdown after having a chocolate bar and that would be chalked up to being perfectly normal. That's not okay.

We just need to find moderation and balance. Don't be that fool who is always giving one-hundred percent to everyone but yourself. Sorry, not sorry. It's human nature to apologize for someone else's misfortune, because we have no control over their situations. Stop that. By apologizing, you are taking responsibility, and thus, control. Empaths, I'm calling you out. Taking on someone's negative energy isn't good for your health. We've learned how to turn it on. Now you need to find a way to turn it off.

If you haven't tried decompression and want some help, here's a spell to do every once in a while when you feel overwhelmed by other people's shit.

Empath Decompression

Supplies:
Blue Candle
Bowl of water
Lapis Lazuli
Salt

Instruction:

Set up the candle in the center of your sacred space, placing a dish of salt to the left and a bowl of water to the right. Lapis lazuli is the stone of the goddess Inanna, a powerful Sumerian deity that holds dominion over the seas and the heavens. She is known to be called on in relation to sex, desire, justice, and healing.

We use blue to represent the healing power of water, and the salt and water as libation. Before the chant, light the candle and meditate for a moment to breathe and gather your intentions. Imagine rolling tides at your feet and the scent of salt water. Picture grains of sand between your toes as the tides grab at you. Feel the wind pull you forward and relieve you of the burdens of others you carry. Let the waters cleanse you.

Either place the lapis lazuli into the bowl of water, or if you have the stone set in jewelry, wear it. As you chant, sprinkle the salt into the water. When you are done, scry into the water and look at your reflection to re-affirm yourself.

<u>Chant</u>:

"Goddess of the seas, the skies, the night
Inanna, I call unto you tonight

As the sea, so the sky
These tears aren't mine I cry

As above, so below
Relieve me of this woe
This is pain I do not own"

Next, it's time to face the 'D word'. Get your head out of the gutter. We're talking about *doubt*. In order to get your shit together, you need to sit down and divorce doubt. If you want that vampiric presence to finally leak free from your pores, your confidence needs to be greater than your doubt.

For any spell to work, you must first believe in it. And if you have a hard time believing in miracles, then start by looking at the facts.

Is what you want within the realm of possibilities? Is your life goal to win the lottery or to be a good mom at the end of the day? You need to get rid of the ideas of luck and chance and turn your probability into something distinctive.

Make sure your goals are within the scope of possibility, and glamour will ensure they come to fruition. But think of it like the rubber band effect. If you stretch the rubber band too far, it's going to snap. You can't break reality, but you can make waves in it.

Doubt births itself from failure. You need to reframe that into determination. If you fall, get up. Brush off the bullshit. You've got this. Failure is a great achievement because it's the result of *trying*. If all you hold is doubt, you will never have a chance at success.

If you aren't able to meditate your way out of feeling drained and hopeless, it's okay to ask for help. While the craft is therapeutic, it unfortunately doesn't replace the benefits of therapy. If therapy hasn't worked in the past, try again. Finding the right therapist can be as taxing as finding the perfect partner. You need to be compatible to have a circle of trust.

In essence, I can pep talk you all day. But if you can't see how great you are, no one is going to change that perspective for you. *You* need to be ready to change. Ready to see your flaws, quirks, and gifts for what they are—and be thankful for the awesome package of you that you've become.

If this all seems like too much, try skipping to the next section, *Create A Safe Space.*

Create a Safe Space

Just as important as feeling safe in your own skin is feeling comfortable in your surroundings. There are several factors that contribute to our mental health and the effectiveness of our glamour magick. Some of the most important contributions are having a space that is clean and tidy, having a place that is comfortable for our well-being, and allowing our personality to shine through.

We stress about our house being messy, but we also stress about the work required to clean it. We've all been there. Most of us don't have the luxury to have much time at home to relax. Moreover, the little time we do have we don't want to spend scrubbing floors. However, you need to set aside some time. Don't 'half-ass' it.

Having abundance isn't always a good thing. There is such a thing as too much. Take time once a week to do a deep cleaning of your house, and I promise you will not regret it. And if you actually do this once a week, it won't take much time at all.

In order to do effective spell work, you must be able to tune out distractions. Let's face it, if your house is in shambles, that's a huge distraction. You know, I get it. Maybe you have kids, pets, or a messy partner. Nevertheless, it's not about fault. It's about responsibility.

Have you ever wondered why a broom is a sacred symbol of witchcraft? Witches quite literally sweep the bad out of their lives. We take the dust and yeet it off the front porch. How can you expect to get rid of your demons when you don't have the energy to get rid of the dust bunnies?

Depression is a very real thing in our lives. Doing simple things like cleaning and taking care of ourselves can be draining. I'm here to help you tackle bad habits one by one and get back to a comfortable place. Maybe taking an entire Saturday to clean your house isn't on the agenda. Let's do one room at a time. We'll start small with the bathroom. Take an hour and scrub it from top to bottom. Give yourself something to be proud of. Everyone deserves a safe and comfortable home.

Now that we have a clean space, let's get back to spell work. Ritual baths are a very important component of glamour magick. There is no right or wrong way to do one. Like how the broom literally sweeps the dirt out of our house, the ritual bath literally cleans the dirt off our bodies. This particular magick cleanses our soul and hearts of all the negative energy we have lingering.

Ritual baths are best done in the evening under moonlight, but simply in the evening is also fine. Some ideas for things to have in and around your bath are candles, washes, salts, herbs, and crystals. I like to indulge in wine and bubbles, as well. If you haven't done this before, you're probably wondering what a wash is. It's like an essential oil, but with water as a base. Most washes are multi-purpose and can be added as a solution to wash surfaces or to your bathwater.

There is a long history of ritual baths being used in practice. It goes as far back as Cleopatra bathing in milk, honey, and roses to remain young and beautiful. Elizabeth Bathory bathed in the blood of virgins to retain youthful allure. (I wouldn't recommend using Bathory as a role model. Not to mention that there are other ingredients a lot easier to obtain than virgins these days.)

In a practical sense, the ability to bathe wasn't as easy back in the day. People didn't have the luxury of bathing every day, which adds to the sacredness of including ritual during bath time. In the modern day, we focus on the healing properties of water.

You can make your own wash, but I suggest grabbing a bottle online or from a local metaphysical shop, as they are inexpensive. But if you can get your hands on some fresh or dried natural ingredients, you will have a much easier time infusing your personal energy into the wash.

There are many scents and purposes for each recipe. There are some to awaken psychic prowess, to increase your income, to un-cross, and even some to elicit love. I'm going to recommend rose water since we're trying to cater to self-love in this case.

Get some white tea lights or some pink and red votives and then douse them in rose oil. Sprinkle any of your favorite herbs, flowers, woodchips, or tea leaves you have lying around your altar and kitchen. I like to use licorice root, lemon balm, jasmine, rose petals or hips, and hibiscus.

Cling to your intuition and use herbs you are drawn to and that help you relax. We want to utilize these ingredients not just at the base of your candles, but also in your bath. To prevent messes, you can wrap them in a cheesecloth or even tie a string around a coffee filter and let it sit in the tub like a tea bag. To me, pouring the loose herbs in is worth the minor mess to clean up later; just be sure to invest in a drain stopper to prevent clogging the pipes.

Rose quartz and clear quarts are good crystals to decorate your tub with for the ritual. They will absorb the energy you're manifesting for a boost later. Think of it like an energy shot. Next, find an incense that compliments the wash and oils you've chosen. You don't want to overwhelm your senses, as that could cause headaches and vertigo. So be careful on what you decide to add to your mix.

During the ritual, you aren't doing much speaking. Your goal is to manifest love and confidence. If you have a deity in mind, you can welcome them to your rite, but in my opinion, this glamour is very personal. Ritual baths are a great place to meditate and to be comfortable in your skin. Use the aromatherapy we've added to your advantage, as well as deep breathing techniques to absorb the steam.

When I am done, I usually invoke a deity like Aphrodite using mirror magick and godform. Mirror magick involves using a mirror as a scrying or oracle tool. While godform magick involves a level of invocation in which you merge your spirit into that of the deity you're working with. It's a form of possession and should only be done with those with whom you have developed a relationship with.

Godform is a type of glamour because you are embodying the characteristics of the deity. Relatable to godform, Wiccans call this practice drawing down the moon, specifically calling the triple goddess into them. In Wicca, this is typically performed by a high priest or priestess.

If you want to try making your own ritual bath wash, you have options. When I make my own, I simmer my ingredients over the stovetop or in a small batch using my tea ball. If you go with the simmer method, you can put loose ingredients in a stockpot or saucepan, or use a coffee filter tied off with twine. If you throw in raw ingredients, just be sure to have a mesh strainer.

When you have your ingredients in the pot, pick out your favorite wooden spoon. This is the wand of the kitchen. The magick infusion starts with stirring. Stir clockwise in most cases, unless the intent of your bath is an uncrossing. In that case, stir counterclockwise.

The water you choose to boil is also important. You could use water that you've previously blessed. You could use moon water or water local to your land from lakes or the ocean. Salt water would be good for working with Aphrodite, for those fortunate enough to live near an ocean. If not, you can always add some pinches of salt and it will get the job done.

If you have the option of cooking over a fire, do so for the wash. There's just something a little more magickal about working over an open flame rather than an electric range. It puts us back to the cauldron stirring days of our roots.

I recently went to my local Pagan Pride and met a witch, Lady Heka, who incorporated baths into her practice, and she shared her methods with me. She took a small tin tub and massaged fresh herbs in the water. She explained that to her, the more she worked her energy into the herbs, the more powerful the magick would be. Another brilliant tip was lighting a candle in the tub she worked the herbs into. She used a glass encased candle and literally could put fire inside of water. When it burned out, she was ready to use the wash.

This last tip from Lady Heka is, in my opinion, the most useful. The idea of a ritual bath always sounds nice. Probably always a good idea. But when your energy is low and you're exhausted, sometimes you need to use the instant recipe instead of making one from scratch. Sometimes you just can't wait. No fear. There's a solution. Take those pre-made teas that you have sitting in your cupboard and give them some life. Take three to five tea bags and tie them to your shower head. Meditate and speak your intent. This is a ritual shower for those on the go.

Here is an example of a glamour bath ritual I recently performed. It has multiple steps. This is a glamour to revive a lost or dead love. If you have a presence on TikTok, you may have seen me post a fragment of this ritual there.

Glamour Bath Ritual

Supplies:
Rose of Jericho
Water dish
Matches
Three chime candles
A closable box or jar
Love talisman

Instruction:
Procure the three candles: one for intuition, one for spirit, and one for love. I chose purple, silver, and pink to represent each, respectively. Next, pick out a talisman to represent the love between you and the target. I have a howlite stone that's shaped into a heart. I used this and wrapped it in a scarlet cloth and anointed it with rose oil and bergamot oil. You can prepare your talisman however you want. It can be something special between you and the target.

Put the talisman into the box when you are ready.
You won't see it for a while. Next, take your water
dish and fill it with clean water. Place it on top of
the box, or if you chose a jar, behind the jar. Cradle
the rose of Jericho. You want to infuse your intent
into it. All of your love and determination to make
your love blossom again. When you've meditated
with it for a moment, place it in the water dish.

Take the (silver) candle that represents spirit and
place it in the middle of the box or top of the
mason jar and light it. If you are using chimes, you
can light the base of the candle and let the hot wax
drip on the surface you want to place it. Hold the
candle steady for a few seconds until it hardens.

Chant:

"I call to spirit to lift me up
To fill my empty cup
To remind me of abundance and love"

Instruction:
This is your personal growth representation. It
takes two to make things work. This is your healing
and motivation. Next, light your (purple) intuition
candle to the left.

Chant:

"I call upon my third eye
To show that love is not blind
It's here in front of me
And me for thine eyes to see"

Instruction:
The final candle is (pink) representation of love. We use pink instead of red to pull out the lust factor. The aggression. We want to be soft but not subtle. Pink is a good choice when re-kindling love.

Chant:

"I call upon the gods above
I call upon all of your love
Infuse the light of love in me
And may my target come back to me"

Instruction:
Now, safely add your essence into the dish with the rose of Jericho. I use a few drops of blood. You can use saliva or semen/vaginal fluids as well. Let the candles burn out and leave the rose of Jericho to bloom. When it blooms, your spell has fully manifested. Wait a few days for it to fully expand. I chose three days.

Then remove the bowl from your altar and the rose. Strain the water into a container to use in your next ritual bath. I also added rose petals, salt, rose oil, lavender oil, and bergamot oil to the mix. Take a ritual bath to cleanse yourself and to seal the work you've done. Once clean, you can remove the talisman from the box and try to keep it close to you for at least the following week after the spell.

The last step for creating a safe space is to put your personality into it. Don't fall in line with what's traditional, conventional, or normal. Normal is boring. If you're a plant person, go ham and fill your patio with exotic plants and macramé. If you like video games, start designing the PC setup of your dreams. Your space should be a reflection of who you are. Somewhere you can seek solace from a hard day at work.

Don't hide your altar in a box. Display it proudly above your fireplace or a freestanding shelf. Your herbs don't have to be hidden away. Place them proudly in your kitchen. Compartmentalization isn't a task you should have to do at home. You should not have to sacrifice pieces of yourself for your family, friends, or anyone.

Another important part of glamour magick is a sense of pride. It's all about presence. Illusion. Give the illusion that you have your shit together.

What you feel is directly going to influence people around you. It's a win/win. If you've worked with magick for a while, it's easy to tell when people around you practice. Everyone gives off a specific energy. In addition, those that practice the craft give off a heightened dose of that energy.

Though with a glamour spell, even those who don't practice the craft will noticeably pick up on those changes and vibrations you're giving. That is, if you want to. Create a mood that lingers. You want someone to walk into your sacred space and *feel*. You want to control that vibration, whether it be to relax, to be happy, or maybe even to dance.

Simmer Pot Recipe

To help set the mood for your space, try creating a simmer pot. It can be before you have guests over or to unwind after a long day. Aromatherapy has so many benefits.

Supplies:
Apple
Cranberries
Orange
Star anise
Cinnamon sticks
Pot
Kitchen knife

Instruction:
Start by filling a pot halfway with water and put your stovetop between medium and medium-high. Next, slice your apple and orange. Size and cut style don't matter. We just don't want to throw the entire fruit in the pot. You can, but I find that doesn't work as well.

If you feel wasteful using the entire fruit, feel free to just use scrap the peel from the orange or the core from the apple. You will still achieve the same goal. You can even strain this into a tea when you are done.

Now, add a handful of cranberries and sparingly drop in cinnamon sticks and star anise. You should start to smell the aroma wafting through your home once the pot begins to simmer. Hence, simmer pot. Because this is an offering to your home to keep your space sacred and safe, be sure to give permission to the hearth to accept the offering.

Chant:

"Thank you, Vesta, for these walls
Both in form and spirit
I call you hence to take libation
And thank you for protection"

You can let a simmer pot run all day, but be sure to monitor and add water when it gets low. You can also re-use your ingredients by storing them in the fridge the next day. For safety reasons, don't leave your simmer pot unattended or on while asleep.

When we first learn about witchcraft, we are all overstimulated by people telling us to cleanse and purify everything. I know you're sick of it. But after doing all this work to make your home comfortable, you need to seal in that feeling with a cleanse. We don't want shadows to linger without permission.

There are plenty of ways to cleanse a home. Some people use sage and waft it through the house. Some people just throw it in as a side note after a ritual to cleanse their space. Like everything in glamour, let's make it a little more personal. We are going to make a concoction. Get out the mop and bucket, because we're going to scrub the negative energy away.

You can clean out an old jug with whatever brand name of floor cleaner you typically use. Alternatively, your local dollar store will have a variety of storage selections for what we're about to make. All you need for this cleaner is equal parts white vinegar diluted with water.

General Purpose Wash

Like the wash you would use in a ritual bath, this can also be used as a cleaner for your floors, walls, and windows. You may not want to use rose water as your preferred scent, but you are more than welcome to! I would personally use something infused with citrus that has a sweet orange scent, lemon balm, or bergamot.

Replace a portion of your water with a wash of your choice; these usually come in about eight-ounce containers. Instead of a wash, add a few drops of your favorite essential oil to the mix. You can even let fruit steep in your cleaning solution for a few days for an extra fresh scent.

After you make the solution, bless it. We are going to make this solution work for us, rather than us chanting over every square inch of our home. Here is an example.

<u>Chant</u>:

"I add water to refresh
And vinegar to cleanse
My home will smell citrus fresh
And inviting to new friends

With this wash I declare
Demons have no place here
Bad energies beware
With this I cleanse all fear"

Now that our space is safe, clean, and has our energy put into it, it's time to meet your hearth spirits. Your hearth spirit or deity, however you choose to see them, is vital to the structure and stability of your home, family, and domestic life.

In Greek mythology, Hestia is the name of this guardian. (Or in Roman mythology, Vest, like who we gave thanks to with our simmer pot) She is the flame on your altar and watches over your sacrifices. This also means she is permitted a share of all sacrifices presented in your hearth. This is her tax for the protection of your homestead and family.

While the hearth collects taxes and leftovers from your libations to other spirits, she is also deserving of her own recognition. If you make friends with your hearth, she will be more apt to protect you and uphold your sacred space.

Hestia traditionally favors young calves for her sacrifices. Please don't go kill Farmer John's cow. Spare Hestia some raw meat from the grocery store. Dedicate a small shelf and dish just for her. She also enjoys wine, oil, and water on her altars.

When giving thanks at the altar of the hearth, I like to call out the Homeric Hymn to Hestia, a goddess of the hearth. Next time you give an offering to your hearth spirit, try repeating the following chant:

"XXIX to Hestia

"Hestia, in the high dwellings of all, both deathless gods and men who walk on earth, you have gained an everlasting abode and highest honor: glorious is your portion and your right. For without you mortals hold no banquet, — where one does not duly pour sweet wine in offering to Hestia both first and last. And you, slayer of Argus, Son of Zeus and Maia, messenger of the blessed gods, bearer of the golden rod, giver of good, be favorable and help us, you and Hestia, the worshipful and dear. Come and dwell in this glorious house in friendship together; for you two, well knowing the noble actions of men, aid on their wisdom and their strength. Hail, Daughter of Cronos, and you also, Hermes, bearer of the golden rod! Now I will remember you and another song also."
(Homer & Evelyn-White)

Hearth Stones

Now the fun part. We're doing arts and crafts. Take out your acrylic paint and march out your front door. We're doing a favored pastime of witches around the world: collecting rocks.

This rock is preferably one found on your property. If you have none, it's okay to scope out your neighborhood. If you live in an apartment, just search around the complex. Just a bit of a tip: Those beautiful, shiny white rocks replacing the garden at your neighbor's house? Yeah, it's best to leave those alone.

You want to find rocks that preferably have at least one smooth side. A perfect size would be ones that fit nicely in your palm. Once you have three, four, or more and before your neighbor's get suspicious, it's time to head back to your hearth.

We are going to dedicate these rocks to our hearth. To do that, you will place sigils on them, infusing them with glamour to protect your house and to honor your hearth. And when we have a nice little collection, you are going to place them close to your crossroads, or traditionally, somewhere near your front door.

Lay out your finds on the table. Don't touch the paint; we're not ready for that yet. First, we need to make a grocery list of concise but powerful sentences and phrases that represent our intent.

Get out your favorite notebook or grimoire and brainstorm the types of energy you want your hearth to have. I'll give a basic example:

MAY THOSE WHO ENTER DO NO HARM.

There are several ways to compose a sigil. You can put your letters in a circle and draw lines connected to the consonants. Or in chaos magick, the most popular way is to start by crossing out all the vowels in your sentence, along with any duplicate consonants. You should have something like this:

MAY TH~~OSE~~ W~~HO~~ ~~ENTER~~ D~~O~~ ~~NO~~ ~~HARM~~.

I find it ironic that 'harm' is completely crossed out here. We're already subconsciously manifesting this sigil! So, here's what we're left with:

MYTHWNRD

Now, this part may be difficult for some. We have to turn on our imagination. We are going to turn these letters into our own sigil. All a sigil is, is a unique symbol of power. In The Lesser Key of Solomon, sigils were first identified as names of angels and demons. As time evolved them and chaos magick adopted them into practice, we in turn began to utilize them for so much more.

Sigils work because they tap into our subconscious mind. We aren't simply reading or regurgitating a chant or phrase. We are putting power into a symbol. Think about it; the ankh, pentacle, Celtic cross, and triquetra would have no power if we didn't put our energy into them.

Don't focus too hard on trying to make your sigil aesthetically pleasing. Just draw what comes naturally. Combine lines, spin your paper as you're drawing. It just has to be unique. And as you're birthing this sigil, manifest your sacred phrase and your intentions into existence.

I'll do my best to draw an example, so you have reference. Don't judge. Once you have one sigil down, make as many as you want. And when you are confident with your energy and intentions, you can then make them permanent and paint them on the rocks. When painting, keep in mind color coordination to further manifest your intent.

Most glamour spells focus on this high energy and love, however, the original glamours were simply about deception. In a way, that's still true. You are lying to yourself about your feelings until you manifest positivity and truth that overcomes those demons. But you could use glamour to not be seen or noticed. Not *literally* invisible, however, merely overlooked. We'll go over that in our next section, *Masking*.

MAY THOSE WHO ENTER DO NO HARM

Masking

Glamour magick isn't all about getting attention. Sometimes it's used to be left the heck alone, as the fae preferred. Like shielding, masking is just another way to stay out of sight and protect yourself. To mask, you need to put yourself into a state of meditation at will. You can accomplish this through conventional meditation techniques and regulating the chakras. On the other hand, you can simply push your energies outward like a shield and clear your mind.

You are allowed to have personal space. You are entitled to not be goggled at and prodded if you don't want to be. Masking is usually defined as a coping mechanism or something that's done by people with insecurities, but it doesn't have to be that way.

People mask for all sorts of reasons. If I'm having issues with anxiety and don't want to worry anyone or cause a scene, I simply revert into myself and mask. I don't want to deal with questions and the inventible asking if I'm okay fifty times. Sometimes we just need space to heal, and we're not always in the right place and the right time.

Use your extremities to tighten your muscles and imagine that you're magnetic, polar to those around you. Don't look directly into people's eyes; instead, try looking *through* them. Imagine yourself with a dull yellow and gray aura to repel anything or anyone that tries to come your way.

If you intentionally need to enter a stressful situation, there are some preparations you can take. When choosing my foundation, I use a pale tone. I am masking into an ethereal energy. I wear my hair down. I cover my skin by wearing leggings or sweats and hoodies. Wear nude glosses and lipsticks.

For crystals, use ones like onyx, obsidian, and tourmaline for grounding and shielding. Use smoky quartz and calcite to represent passing by unnoticed. Your goal is to camouflage and not draw attention.

If you choose to wear a scent, use earthy tones like patchouli and sandalwood. However, use these lightly, as just a few drops are very potent. You are using scent and aesthetic to deter, not to attract negative attention and annoyed glances.

Another use for masking is if you're focused on a project or for when you're at work. It will help you stay in the zone and on task. It's the perfect tool for us procrastinators. As I write this book, I'm currently in a public place, and I'm masking.

Glamour isn't about ritual as much as it is about perception. It's a big picture concept, and many witches that learn via strict ritual practice and high magick can have a hard time grasping simply controlling the energies within and around you. It actually took me years to realize that I didn't need to cast a circle for every spell or always call to each element and hold an athame to the sky under a full moon. Magick can be done any time and in any place. The best tool you will ever have is your willpower.

I have a lot of physical scars from my past, especially on my legs. This is never something I thought I would talk about to anyone, let alone blast it into the world in a book. Only a handful of friends and partners know this and how it affects me. I hate showing off my legs in a dress or skirt and always cover up with leggings. I'm extremely self-conscious in my bathing suit, being unable to hide those scars in that situation.

When I go out to the lake or to a pool party, I use masking to keep attention off of my legs. Now, it's a lot more difficult to only mask a certain part of you. Just because I don't want attention on my scars doesn't mean I want to hide in the shadows.

To do this masking to only conceal a feature, you will need to meditate. I use traditional mediation, visualizing my chakra into colors for each part of my body. When I want to use those chakras, I imagine color-coordinated light emanating from my bodily areas that control those chakras.

My legs are associated with my root chakra, which is red. This is the chakra of grounding. I don't want to lessen my grounding, merely alter perception. When I envision my root chakra, I also alter my throat chakra, which is blue. It's the chakra of healing. Before I ever enter the water, I'm imaging these spiritual waves masking the scars on my legs. That's how to bend your chakras to cast glamour.

Mask Crafts

If you are not in a stressful situation and have a chance for privacy, it's a good idea to practice masking before you need it. Whether you want to mask to slip into the shadows or to simply put on a persona, this craft is a fun exercise. We are going to make a literal mask.

Supplies:
Mirror
Construction paper
Scissors
Hole puncher
Twine
Marker
Optional: Glitter and other decorative additions

Instruction:
This is a fun activity that can be changed up easily depending on why you're masking. It can be done with the whole family to teach your kids about confidence. Have them make one with you, and it will teach them spiritually and metaphorically how to do masking without the physical representation.

Use color coordination. If you are masking to show confidence, use a bright color like yellow. If you want to practice 'shutting off' and grounding, use black construction paper.

Take your construction paper and fold it in half like a card. We are going to draw our mask shape from the side where it's folded. It can be in any shape you want. Use your marker and let it be organic. Just know that you have to start and end your line on the side of the paper that has the fold/crease. This way, when you cut on your line, you have a symmetrical shape when you open it up. (Think of those heart-shaped Valentine's Day cards you made as a kid.)

About an inch from the crease, draw a circle or design that you will later cut as an eyehole. Take your scissors and cut around your outline. Before you unfold, grab your hole punch and punch through the inside of where you drew the eyes. This way, you have a place to feed the scissors through to cut. Carefully cut the eyes out. Then unfold your paper and make corrections as needed to your design.

After you are happy with the general shape of your mask, punch a hole in each end. Cut two even pieces of twine and tie a knot through both holes. Use this time to draw designs like runes, sigils, or symbols on your mask. You can even write your intentions on the mask. Decorate and add glitter if you wish. Here's an example chant to mask for confidence:

Chant:

"When I put this mask upon my face
My timid self will go away
My confidence will shine like stars

And won't leave when I discard this veil"

While most masking is done on yourself, you can also place masks on others. You have the right to mask people that oppress you. We've all been in a situation where there have been rumors spread about us. If someone is taking the time to put their energy into shaming you, you should not feel bad about masking them.

If ignored, rumors will grow. If someone is really adamant about crashing tides into your life, they will try to have your friends and family turn against you. That's what people who manipulate others do. Those with sociopathic tendencies will use you until you no longer serve their purpose. Then they will find another vessel. You simply get in their way of manipulating others once you have the potential to oust them.

For masking another, you will need to come full force with your willpower. It's yours against theirs.

In sealing and chants, repetition is key. Take a photo of them and cross out their mouths. Chant something like "The boy who cries wolf cries to himself. No others come when he cries for help." I suggest using a specific name in these mantras.

For coordinating colors, use black. Black candles. Black ink. Black clothing. Hold a funeral for their words and force them to eat them. After you've spoken and written your mantras, burn them in a fire safe container.

Other reasons to mask include protecting your family. Children are susceptible to outside influences. Mask them so that they stay safe. You have to realize that not everyone has good intentions, even those you share similar vibrations with.

I learned this many years ago while attending a Pagan fair, as I always do. These events are something that I introduced my daughter to early on in her life. One time, I had a conversation with a vendor who practiced Hoodoo. She had her child with her, and she seemed concerned.

We talked for a while, and she explained how she would shield her kid before coming to any event. People even unintentionally have a habit of consuming others' energy, especially those who give off strong psychic energy. Children are vulnerable.

While I always have at least a thin-layered mask in public, it's not something I think about. From that point forward, I made it a point to mask my daughter for those types of events. Even as she blossoms into her own, beautiful witch self, it's my responsibility to protect her from those outside energies until she's old enough to interpret what's safe to let in.

Masking isn't always about pushing people away. Sometimes it's having a different persona. People with gender dysphoria may use masking to feel more comfortable in their own skin. An introvert in a customer service position masks when they clock in for the day, so they put on a smile and bask in that extrovert glamour. Masking is when you have to appear professionally in court, but on the inside, you're a nervous wreck. So, you take on the qualities of Nemesis to have confidence and to be sure justice is served. There are many reasons we may want to walk in someone else's shoes for the day or to temporarily restructure ourselves.

Mirrors are a useful tool for masking. When we look into a mirror, we see ourselves, and oftentimes we see through perspective, even though our physical image doesn't change. We look in the mirror and instantly gravitate toward flaws. But with the positive affirmations we discussed earlier, we also know how to combat that destructive self-talk.

To use mirrors in ritual, all you need to do is envision what you want to manifest. Even if it's something as simple and mundane as wishing a zit away. Or something as complex as shifting your aura. I want you to do an exercise utilizing mirror magick.

Mirror Masking

- Step 1 Find some privacy. This exercise is most comfortably done in your safe space.
- Step 2 Find a large mirror to use that you can see your full body in. It doesn't have to be dedicated.

- Step 3 Get naked. Don't argue. This step is important.
- Step 4 Make and announce a list of facts about yourself. Not opinions. I don't want you telling yourself how fat you think you are or how oddly shaped. State obvious things, like freckles on your face, brown eyes, ten fingers, ten toes.
- Step 5 Be honest. Not brutal. We are giving constructive criticism. There's a reason you're masking. Make a list of things you want to work on with yourself. These could be physical, social, mental, or spiritual attributes.
- Step 6 Announce a list of things you want to mask. Say them one by one and speak them into existence.

Traditionally, masking was also a very literal concept. If you practice the sabbats, you are aware of Samhain's history and how it's leaked into social cultures today around the world, for example in Halloween. Masks were worn in rituals on Samhain to ward off evil spirits. These rituals were specifically performed on Samhain because it was believed this was the day the veil was the thinnest between the corporal and ethereal realms.

Along with people, objects were also glamoured to ward evil spirits from the hearth. Did you know that jack-o'-lanterns were traditionally carved from turnips? They are definitely not cute like pumpkins when carved.

When you think of Halloween and Samhain, there are many associations. We can taste it. Smell it. Feel it. The energy is just... different. In a good way. Your entire environment is manipulated. Let me set the mood and show you through glamour.

The aroma of pumpkin spice bread and zucchini muffins fill the home. Autumn-colored candles kindle, the wax smelling of leftover batter. The cinnamon besom stands next to the door, welcoming in the good-spirited. This is the heart of the season; this is Samhain.

Celebrating life is the best way to celebrate death. With the thinning of the veil, it is said that spirits of good nature and bad are able to materialize in the physical realm.

During the month of October, I welcome the spirits, usually with bountiful feasts, crafts, and other offerings, depending on the tradition I am following. Being the last harvest of the year, Samhain reminds me that the death of the year draws near. This is the one night that shines brighter than day.

Bury the live
Let ashes rise
In death, you'll revive
The old and the wise

The trees are bare, and Gaia has painted a watercolor scheme on the ground below. Aether whistles throughout the obsidian night, calling for spirits and tossing about leaves. Frightened children hide under covers, proselytized by Hollywood's displays and their dread of the unknown.

The forgotten guardian stands fiercely on my porch. The umber-colored gourd brawls with the uninvited spirits, warding them away. The hollow creature waits in valor for any that wish to contend from the void. The jack-o'-lantern can bare many faces: animals, abstract art, or symbols of the season. Though each flame is all the same; it is represented as its soul. The taller and brighter the flame, the more powerful the guardian is. I worry if the flame falters, peril comes close.

Dark shadows are cast upon the igniter if a candle is snuffed the night of All Hallows' Eve. It is said that curses may come to the family the guardian was sent to protect. There is always a sense of foreboding in the stagnant air when in the presence of an unlit jack-o'-lantern.

Seasons are born
By quarter, they bloom
New is each morn'
From runes of the moon

Maple and sassafras smolder outside, the wood sweet and crisp. Logi ignites his flames toward the sky, extending toward the blood moon; his fire sends chills through the air. The smoke whirls around the circle, along with escaping embers. The fire crackles and hisses, then slightly calms. Drums start to beat, and our hearts start to pound. The ritual begins. Each quarter has a candle and offering, encompassed around the fire.

Cider is passed all around, along with mixtures of autumn's sacred fruits. The sweet elixir is a dose of energy to all who drink. Our ancestors are celebrated for and with; poetry, song, and rites fill the night with good vibes and adrenaline. The circle blurs into the sway of dancers with fervor and grace. The people's energy becomes one in the enchanted eventide, forming a stellar fog of starry night. Above, below, and in-between lay the crossroads to the forever dream.

A web is laced between the branches of birch and elder, their arms extending like arches. Then, when all settles down, I can hear the secrets of the night. I can feel my skin glow and see the moonlight flowing luminously through my veins.

Let chaos be tamed
By Nyx and her childer
As Erebus reigns
Alongside wilder

When it's time to part, I realize the energy is released back to Gaia. A great sense of gravity is lifted and then released. The spirits' clocks have until sunrise, and then the veil lifts until next season. It is hard to tell if it is my body shaking, or the earth beneath my feet. By this time, dew has already been collected on Earth's surface. The plush carpet is a comforting feeling between my toes as Aegir's remnants saturates the air.

Logi's energy is respectfully extinguished, his smoke lifting up to Nyx and Erebus. For a moment, the October air is warm, like Erebus is cloaking me. His dolent embrace reminds me that the spirits have been sent to rest peacefully for another year.

How did that passage make you feel? This is an example of using the senses to trigger a glamour. A common practice to manifest glamour through our senses is to utilize sight. It's a lot easier to envision a future we can physically see.

We are going to mask our self-doubt with this exercise. Instead of focusing on what you want to fix, focus on what you want to manifest. The universe doesn't like the word 'no.' So instead of thinking about things you don't want, try only focusing on things you do. This is masking through your subconscious.

Try making a vision board of short-term and long-term goals. You want your board to define you, so I can't give you a spell or recipe on how to craft one. Mine would include neon colors, glitter, and rainbows to attract the eye. I would write mantras I want to manifest like 'More Money,' 'New Friends,' and 'Book Deal.' I would put pictures of book art, friends, family, and anything I associate with happiness.

The goal of a vision board is to make goals that are obtainable and within your reach. You want to put it somewhere you can look at each day, and have it drilled into your subconscious when you're not looking at it Learn more about glamouring your environments in my next section, *Attract Energy, Not People.*

Attract Energy, Not People

Everyone wants to find their soulmate, their twin flame, their person. But even us witches make mistakes with our intuition. We're still clumsy. And the person for us yesterday isn't necessarily the person for us today. Therefore, when I perform love spells to attract, I don't pick out a person and force them against their will. Instead, I manifest attraction and the willpower to draw energies toward me that I desire and would mesh with.

Instead of inscribing names into your spellwork, try attributes, desires, emotions, and sacred symbols. We mentioned using candles earlier and writing at the base of them in cord cutting. My favorite form of inscription uses paper birch bark and ink. I always keep a stash of birch bark in a chest. Trees all have their own spirits and used to be worshipped as their own respective deities.

Birch is a sacred tree in many ways. It symbolizes rebirth and the crossroads of life and death. It also represents a portal to the underworld and other realms. Most importantly, birch represents transformation and growth. Transcendence.

"Beneath you birch with silver bark
And boughs so pendulous and fair,
The brook falls scattered down the rock:
and all is mossy there!

And there upon the moss she sits,
The Dark Ladié in silent pain
The heavy tear is in her eye,

And drops and swells again."

(Coleridge, 1772-1834)

First, start by obtaining the bark from a paper birch tree. Be sure to thank the tree for its sacrifice. Write what you desire on the tan side of the bark. It can be written with a normal pen, but it's more fun to use a quill and ink. If you buy your ink separately, you can also infuse other things into it, as you would with essence magick. I have a bottle of red ink with a couple drops of blood to make my spells more potent. It's a clean, safe, and simple way to incorporate blood magick into any rite.

After you've written your desires upon the bark, to seal the spell, you throw it in flames. It could be a candle dish, your fireplace, or a bonfire. Just make sure you practice this rite in a safe place.

I usually use my mortar to burn the birch and afterward burn some loose incense in the pot with remnants of the birch. For glamours of attraction or cleansing, I also use rose petals, licorice root, and orris root.

Here are some words of power to give you ideas about what you can manifest:

Wealth
Happiness
Longevity
Friendship
Trust

Glamourous Mediums

There are plenty of ways to manifest glamour spells that are more creative and specific to you and your hobbies. Anything in the arts can be infused with glamour. Let's take painting as an example. Think of your paintbrush as a wand. Every time you load color onto your brush, do so with purpose.

When you dab into cardamom yellow, imagine strolling through the tall grass in summer with only the wind between your feet and the dirt. Imagine strolling down a boardwalk at sunset as children pass by laughing, lovers stroll along hand-in-hand, intoxicated by one another, and street performers have the time of their lives doing what they love.

Purposefully load your phthalo green and imagine getting a raise at work through a performance review, getting a new business opportunity or job offer, or your bank account increasing.

You are manifesting emotion and desire through your art. The energy you put into your art, you will get back in return once your spell comes to fruition. It may not be in the abundance or obviousness you wanted, but take notice of small wins. Display your art somewhere that you will be reminded of it often. Maybe that's in your living room or perhaps in your office. You can even gift your glamour to someone else through these physical objects.

Art can come in many forms. My writing is an art. The ability to weave words into a story. The ability to create thoughts, feelings, and desires from simple letters on a page. This is the perfect conduit for glamour. My encouragement to you is to conduct glamour on paper. Although you aren't fondling ink on these pages from blood, sweat, and tears, you metaphorically are.

Art is meant to leave an impression long after it's gone. Our intent with art is to share our passion with those around us. It's therapeutic. It doesn't even have to be visual. Music is another great method of using glamour. Whether it be your vocal cords or an instrument, sound is a wonderful sense to utilize for glamour spells.

My favorite witchy celebrity is Stevie Nicks from Fleetwood Mac. She is a prime example of someone who uses glamour as a performer. Ever since her song *Rhiannon* in 1976 about the Welsh goddess, Nicks has received flack and countless rumors about being a witch. Witchcraft in the seventies wasn't as accepted as it is today. As a matter of fact, it's still not fully accepted.

Stevie has denied claims in many interviews about being a witch. It's rumored that she admitted in a podcast that she practiced Italian witchcraft known as Stregheria. The bottom line is, whatever she chooses to identify as is her business. If she is a witch, she has the right to come out on her own terms, or not at all.

Witch or not, Nicks has an undeniable stage presence. Stevie and her bandmate Lindsey Buckingham were a force not to reckon with on stage, especially after their public breakup. The power of love and heartbreak brought the breath of life into the glamour of her stage presence.

Listen to *Landslide* and imagine manifesting change in your life in regard to letting go of a partner. Life is short. We don't have the time to question love, just live in it. And if you're not living love, move on. Manifest love and don't try to extract it from a person you've had a history with. Look in the mirror in the sky to find love. It's in yourself, your soul, your heart, your gods.

Listen to *Dreams* and imagine a partner who has broken your trust. Imagine singing that song to them, with them, inches from them in a damp studio. That's the type of energy I want you to bring to your glamours. Bring confidence, truth, and boldness. Manifest the truth you deserve for closure.

For another example of music in glamour, think of the sirens in *The Odyssey* luring sailors to their death with the beauty of their voices. One of my favorite fictional witch movies is *Hocus Pocus*. Yes, the witches are the bad guys. But they do *bad* so well. When Winnie takes the mic and sings, *I'll Put a Spell on You*, that's an example of using glamour through music.

In real life, we can use songs to get attention from a lover or someone we fancy. Maybe you're in a karaoke bar and you want someone to buy you a drink. Hit you up. Be enamored. You want your voice to slow down time, and you want your target to listen, not only to your words, but the suggestions through your eyes. Eye contact is very important for performers.

When Sarah takes to the sky on her broom and sings *Come Little Children*, that's another example of glamour through music. Of course, this is fiction. Witches don't lure children from their homes and suck out their souls. You know that. Others may not know that but we can still enjoy pop culture and Hollywood's stories all the same.

I used to get very upset when the media misrepresented our culture, but then I realized something. We *are* being represented. Christianity is used as a trope in horror stories all the time. If someone really wants to believe that witches diddle the devil, fly on brooms, and eat babies, it's not our problem to correct that. So, it's also not our job to defend ourselves.

Another art you could use as a medium is the culinary arts. When you prepare a meal for a sabbat, you are bestowing blessings on your family, friends, and coven. Each ingredient is purposeful. When you knead bread, do so by hand. Weave your magick through your fingertips. Massage it with your knuckles.

If you are doing a glamour to attract wealth, brush your bread with a healthy amount of olive oil, parsley, and basil. If you are doing a glamour to attract love, infuse your dough with rose water and fold some dried cherries into the dough. Make a main course of red meat and sear it, so it's rare in the center. If you are doing a glamour to put someone in good health, make a hearty stew. Mindfully dice your potatoes and carrots. Be selective about the bones of your broth.

Infusing glamour into your cooking is for more than just sabbats and Thanksgiving. Put some magick into a bake sale to help your kid with their fundraiser. Make some cookies for your open house with the intention of getting a good offer. Make a hearty breakfast for your family so that they start their days with smiles and determination.

Try spicing up your sex life by including aphrodisiacs in your recipes. A Hollywood example of using food in glamour is the movie *Chocolat* in which Johnny Depp is romanced by a traveling witch who opens up a chocolate shop in town. Townspeople visit her to find a chocolate that will solve all their problems until the mayor accuses her of sin and forbids people of the church from visiting her shop.

Here's a list of ingredients you can throw into your meals to glamour your significant other:

Almonds
Figs
Strawberries
Cherries
Pomegranate

Ginger
Chocolate
Avocado
Chili Pepper or Cayenne

Here is a recipe that is sure to glamour someone that you have your eyes on or perhaps spice things up with a partner. Aphrodisiacs are meant to alter moods and energy. This isn't a guarantee to get someone in bed with you, though it will certainly set a glamour for you to manifest a mood.

Come To Me Chocolate Cake

This chocolate cake is decadent and rich, topped with a homemade raspberry sauce. This delicious dessert is loaded with aphrodisiacs such as chocolate, raspberries, cayenne, and brown sugar. Anyone who takes a bite is sure to be sweet to you.

Ingredients:
- 18oz semi-sweet chocolate
- ½ cup butter
- 5 eggs
- 4tsp brown sugar
- 4tsp flour
- 1tsp cayenne
- 1tsp salt
- 12oz raspberries
- ¼ cup white sugar
- ¼ cup water
- 2 tsp cornstarch
- ½ tsp vanilla extract

<u>Instructions</u>:
Preheat your oven to 425 degrees and grease a nine-inch cake pan. Use a double boiler to combine the chocolate and butter until smooth. Remove from the heat.

In a separate bowl, whisk the brown sugar and eggs together. Slowly add flour, salt, and cayenne to the mix. Take about a quarter of this mixture and combine it into the chocolate sauce, slowly combining the rest until the cake batter is completely mixed.

Pour the mixture into your cake pan and bake for fifteen minutes. Let cool. While the cake is cooling, bring a saucepan to medium heat and add the water, cornstarch, raspberries, and white sugar.

Stir. Next, bring this mixture to a boil and continue to stir, mashing the raspberries. Reduce the heat and allow this to continue to cook for an additional ten minutes. Then remove from the heat and stir in the vanilla extract.

Use this raspberry sauce to drizzle over your chocolate cake and serve it to someone you want to get frisky with.

While preparing the serving, here's a quick spell to infuse into the cake:

<u>Chant</u>:

"Semi-sweet love
Deep in decadence

It's what I dream of
Innocence that melts in your mouth
A confection of affection
I can't go without

Indulge the mystic velvet
Candy-coated sweat
Delicious desire
Dampened fire
Sugar lingers on your lips
Hips bridging for a fix"

Kitchen Blade Dedication

If kitchen witchery is your jam, try dedicating an athame or ritual dagger for kitchen spells. Use this dagger to cut and prepare your ingredients and as a serving knife. Here's a quick spell to dedicate a kitchen knife for ritual purposes. Store it somewhere separate from your other kitchenware. Clean it with cooking oil.

Chant:

"I dedicate this blade
To serve my will
To enchant what's made
With magick instilled"

Glamour magick isn't always over-the-top. Even glamour can be subtle. The easiest glamour spells are those that affect your mundane tasks. Start small with your requests and expect big with your rewards.

Another way to attract energy is to simply take it. Every witch I know has a collection of tiny jars. Go into your stash and grab some jars and labels. This takes canning to an entirely new level. We are going to can your emotions. Label one for anger, sorrow, and happiness.

You can either meditate in order to achieve these emotional states or store the jars for later. It's best to use *raw* emotions. Next time you're angry, I want you to write down things that you hate. Then crumble up the paper and put it in the jar. Next, go outside in a desolate area and scream into the jar. Let out all your anger. Just don't shriek at home and concern the neighbors.

For sorrow, make a list of things that make you sad. Fold the paper nicely and hold it. Then, I want you to let yourself cry. Use the folded paper to soak and catch your tears before placing it in the sorrow jar.

For happiness, write down things that make you happy. You can include photographs or whatever you want. The next part may feel a little strange, but I want you to laugh. Open the jar and make funny noises into it and just laugh. Then seal it up and put it with the rest.

Harvesting energy and storing for later is a great tool for any spell, even outside of the realm of glamour. You never know when you need it. When you're sick, or depressed, or just worn out; now you have options!

And the same way you can store your energy, you can store others'. I won't give a spiel on what's ethical and how to source it. That's on you. But I would recommend making jars to store energy for family members, friends, and partners.

Include in the jar personal effects, photos, hair, nails, blood. This isn't just for cursing, although that certainly is an option. You never know when you'll need to track someone down or help them. Imagine your kid goes missing. Your partner is suddenly very sick. You need to act now, not later. This is why you must always be prepared. Just be sure to label jars discreetly, using symbols you would recognize, sigils, or runes.

For later use, add honey to the jar for a sweetening spell. Add cayenne for curses. Add water for healing. The possibilities are endless. You will be glad you harvested the energy one day.

Deities Who Will Help You Find Your Inner Goddess

This section is to help you find your inner goddess. Throughout this section, we will discuss goddesses that work well in glamour magick, what offerings they like, a little history, and an example of how to work with them.

Aphrodite

I'll start out with the obvious and say that both Aphrodite and Venus are great choices to work with on glamour spells. Greek and Roman mythology are pantheons we have a lot of information and stories preserved from. All of the offerings that Aphrodite loves, you probably already have for your glamour magick. Anything decedent, beautiful, and sweet would make a suitable offering or dedication. I'll make a list below of some that she appreciates:

Rose petals / rose hips / rose oil
Apples / apple incense
Seashells / stones found on a beach
Strawberries
Pomegranate
Chocolate
Rose quartz
Red wines or blushes
Mead
Locally sourced fresh or salt water

Aphrodite has quite an interesting birth story, of which there are two versions. In the first version, she was one of many of Zeus's children. Though in the more popular tale, she was born of sea foam and Uranus's genitals which were thrown into the sea. I guess that's where Aphrodite must have gotten her wild side!

Aphrodite was known to have many lovers. She was put into an arranged marriage with Hephaestus, known to be the ugliest man of Greece, to teach her a lesson on vanity. She, of course, wasn't faithful and followed her heart and gut.

Her love and lust incited wars of jealousy. She held both divine and human lovers. One of her last encounters of seduction was with a human named Paris, which is where the story of the golden apple comes from. Aphrodite had fought for this fruit with Hera and Athena for the title of the fairest in the land.

She came nude to Paris and bribed him with another beautiful woman, Helen of Sparta. The rest is history. This is one of the reasons apples make a perfect offering for Aphrodite.

When inviting Aphrodite to work with me, I like to recite her passage in the *Hymns of Orpheus*. I particularly enjoy the version translated by Thomas Taylor, 1792, below.

"HEAV'NLY, illustrious, laughter-loving queen,

Sea-born, night-loving, of an awful mien;

Crafty, from whom necessity first came,
Producing, nightly, all-connecting dame:
'Tis thine the world with harmony to join,
For all things spring from thee, O pow'r divine.
The triple Fates are rul'd by thy decree,
And all productions yield alike to thee:
Whate'er the heav'ns, encircling all contain,
Earth fruit-producing, and the stormy main,
Thy sway confesses, and obeys thy nod,
Awful attendant of the brumal God:
Goddess of marriage, charming to the sight,
Mother of Loves, whom banquetings delight;
Source of persuasion, secret, fav'ring queen,
Illustrious born, apparent and unseen:
Spousal, lupercal, and to men inclin'd,
Prolific, most-desir'd, life-giving., kind:
Great sceptre-bearer of the Gods, 'tis thine,
Mortals in necessary bands to join;
And ev'ry tribe of savage monsters dire
In magic chains to bind, thro' mad desire.

Come, Cyprus-born, and to my pray'r incline,
Whether exalted in the heav'ns you shine,
Or pleas'd in Syria's temple to preside,
Or o'er th' Egyptian plains thy car to guide,
Fashion'd of gold; and near its sacred flood,
Fertile and fam'd to fix thy blest abode;
Or if rejoicing in the azure shores,
Near where the sea with foaming billows roars,
The circling choirs of mortals, thy delight,
Or beauteous nymphs, with eyes cerulean bright,
Pleas'd by the dusty banks renown'd of old,
To drive thy rapid, two-yok'd car of gold;

Or if in Cyprus with thy mother fair,
Where married females praise thee ev'ry year,
And beauteous virgins in the chorus join,
Adonis pure to sing and thee divine;
Come, all-attractive to my pray'r inclin'd,
For thee, I call, with holy, reverent mind."

(Orpheus & Taylor, 1792)

Before my ritual baths, I like to put out a bowl of moon water containing a floating rose within a circle of salt as an offering for Aphrodite. It's my personal invitation for her to join my rite and bask in my glamour. In return, I ask for her divine power to aid in my magick, especially if I'm feeling dysphoric.

Another powerful poet from ancient Greece that wrote a devotional to Aphrodite was Sappho. Below is a translation from Edwin Marion Cox, 1925:

"Shimmering-throned immortal Aphrodite,
Daughter of Zeus, Enchantress, I implore thee,
Spare me, O queen, this agony and anguish,
    Crush not my spirit

Whenever before thou has hearkened to me—
To my voice calling to thee in the distance,
And heeding, thou hast come, leaving thy father's
    Golden dominions,

With chariot yoked to thy fleet-winged coursers,
Fluttering swift pinions over earth's darkness,
And bringing thee through the infinite, gliding

Downwards from heaven,

Then, soon they arrived and thou, blessed goddess,
With divine continence smiling, didst ask me
What new woe had befallen me now and why,
   Thus I had called thee.

What in my mad heart was my greatest desire,
Who was it now that must feel my allurements,
Who was the fair one that must be persuaded,
   Who wronged thee Sappho?

For if now she flees, quickly she shall follow
And if she spurns gifts, soon shall she offer them
Yea, if she knows not love, soon shall she feel it
   Even reluctant.

Come then, I pray, grant me surcease from sorrow,
Drive away care, I beseech thee, O goddess
Fulfil for me what I yearn to accomplish,
   Be thou my ally."

(Sappho & Cox, 1925)

While we already gave one example of a ritual bath
calling to Aphrodite in the *Creating A Safe Space*
chapter, I will provide another ritual from my
personal grimoire.

Aphrodite Self-Love Glamour

<u>Supplies:</u>
Rose petals
Rose oil

Rose incense

Instruction:
Fill the tub with warm water and disperse the rose
petals as the water runs. Light the incense and soak
in the water. Anoint yourself lightly with rose oil
and rub the rose petals over your skin.

Chant:

"Blessed the heart, the soul, the mind
May in basking love I will find
The beauty and grace in Mother's touch
Unfold my skin, but not too much

Kindle the subtle
Reveal and feel
Let passion grow
Make my skin glow

Aphrodite
I call upon ye
Help me see
The beauty in me"

If you are looking for a masculine Greek
counterpart to call forth, try working with Apollo,
Cupid, or Eros.

Isis

My favorite Egyptian deity, Isis, is a powerful and
strong goddess of love and glamour. Her love story

of Osiris is told in many ways, and each are unique and awe-striking. The original power couple evoked jealously from everyone around them, despite their generosity to share abundance and love. One of those jealous onlookers happened to be the brother of Osiris, Set. In a jealous rage, Set was said to have trapped Osiris in a coffin and tossed him into the Nile.

In response, Isis used a glamour and transformed herself into a bird to search the land for her lover. Many of the Egyptian deities could appear as animals or have features of animals. Osiris's tears flooded the Nile, and from the coffin grew a tree so that his wife may find him. Eventually, Isis found her husband. But Set hadn't planned for this, and his anger grew. He cut up his brother into fourteen pieces and dispersed him around Egypt.

But with perseverance and Isis's power of true love and glamour, she overcame the evilness of her brother-in-law. She successfully found all fourteen pieces of her husband, the last being his genitals. With her power of love and light, she re-animated him and pieced him back together with gold and wax. And for a time, they could embrace again. They indulged in intimacy and thus conceived Horus.

A beautiful ode to their love is the *Burden of Isis.* Try reciting the translation by James Teackle Dennis from 1910. These chants and laments are in honor of Osiris by his wife, Isis, and his sister, Nephthys. Here is a beautiful excerpt of the translation:

"Come in peace because of our love for thee—
come like the breath, like my love at beholding
thee!
My arms are raised for thy protection; love thou
me!
Love thou me in the two orbits of the Realms of
Osiris, full of my pondering about thee!
There thou dost receive a fillet for the hair among
them who dwell therein;
Breezes blow for thee with perfume, oh husband,
elder, lord beloved!"

(Dennis, 1910)

Isis adores anything that's lavish, fragrant, and has
luster. Offer her jewelry and anything with bright
colors. Here's a list of some ideas of what she likes:

Lotus
Jasmine
Colorful fabric
White wine
Citrine
Lapis lazuli
Cedar
Sandalwood
Honey
Grapes

Here's a glamour to cast between you and a lover
so that you may always find each other as Isis
found her lover Osiris. This is an ultimate
dedication to the one you love, so you may find
them in the next life and lives to come. During this

spell, feel free to take on godform of Isis and Osiris by doing an invocation beforehand.

Osiris' May You Always Find Me Seeds

Supplies:
Tree seeds (See instruction for ideas on type of trees)
Watering can
Local dirt
Gardening shovel
Essence from both parties

Instruction:
Like Osiris blossoming into a tree for his lover to find, we are going to plant seeds to symbolize giving a beacon to your soulmate. Which tree you decide to plant and when relies on your geographical location. Birch trees represent transcendence through realms. Dogwood represents loyalty. Oak represents supreme power and stability. Wisteria represents romance. Redwood represents limitless and timeless magick. Think about the type of love you share with your partner and determine which tree spirit best suits your affection with each other.

Do this spell in your yard or in a special outdoor place that holds memories of your love. Lay the cloth on the ground below and kneel in front of your partner. Put the seed packet in the center between both you and your partner. On one side, place the watering can, full of water. On the other side of the seeds, take the gardening shovel and stick in straight into the ground. Next, hold both hands of your partner and say this chant together.

<u>Chant</u>:

"Osiris, give me strength
With your love, bless this place
Within these fertile grounds do lay,
Supple soil, dirt, and clay

To mold our love into these seeds
So, we too, will become this tree

Our love will be a beacon to
Wherever our hearts and no matter our views
My love, I'll find my way back to you"

Now, one of you will pick up the seeds and pour them into your palm. Clasp your hands together while the other takes the shovel and digs a hole in the middle of the space, appropriate for the type of tree you are planting. The person digging the hole will repeat this chant:

"This shovel, my wand
My will, my bond"

Next, place the seeds into the hole. With your bare hands, both you and your partner will cover the seeds with dirt. Pat it down, then both of you should place your hands over the top of the seeds, with each of your hands on top of the other's. Both chant:

"Our love is laced within this land
Our magick flows from the palms of our hands
As our love grows every day
This tree too, will grow with grace"

Remove your hands and meditate as one of you waters the soil. The one who waters the soil should chant:

110

"Water is the blood of the Earth
The flow of death and rebirth"

Next, have both of you prepare your personal essence
and add it to the top of the soil. This is commonly blood,
but can also be tears, sweat, or sexual fluids. Both of
you then chant:

"And with my essence, I do seal
This bond forever, with the turn of the wheel"

Perun

Let's move onto a lesser-known deity, Perun. He is
of Slavic roots and is worshipped as a god of light,
storms, and the living. Perun works well with
glamour magick because of his favorite weapon,
golden apples. They represent vanity, greed, and
destruction - an ultimate weapon. It makes me
wonder if there are parallels to Perun with
Aphrodite and her myths.

Call on Perun when you want to instill greed and
jealousy in others. Here is an ode to Perun from my
Book of Invocations. Infuse your energy into an
apple and gift it to the intended target.

"From the highest branches
Of the grand Oak
The god of witches
The sword of stone

Perun, grant me your power
Perun, share your thunder

I invoke you through my scepter
The devil's finger

Reveal the golden apple
With a burning arrow through it
A treasure one cannot steal
Without disease at one's heel

A bite for me will heal a curse
But a taste from another will do its worst

Perun, show me lightning
Great ruler of the living

See my humble sacrifice
And grant me your light tonight"

Here are some offering ideas for Perun:

Apples
Oak
Gold
Stone
Bread
Meat
Corn
Grain
Amber
Rainwater

The deities that are lesser known and that we don't
have much literature on are the easiest to work
with because they have less demand, they have
more time for mundane requests, and are more
apt to have an open ear.

Much of your information on deities like Perun will come from your gnosis. Your gnosis is the path of your personal studies of witchcraft. It is the insight you gain from your third eye and working with your own twists on rituals and with deities.

Lilith

Next on the list of deities that thrive in glamour is Lilith. Lilith is known for her beauty, cunning, darkness, and her persuasiveness. I'm going to take you somewhere you may not expect in a book on witchcraft. We're going to discuss a bible story. Even if you've never studied Christianity, you know something of the mythos between Adam and Eve, with those two being the first humans created by Yahweh.

Although the bible doesn't name Lilith in the creation story, it is hinted that she is the serpent and was Adam's first wife. Lilith used a glamour to disguise herself as one of her familiars, the snake, and tempted Eve with persuasion to eat her fruit. I translate that as Lilith saying: *Fuck men. Adam is a jerk. I think you're kind of cute. Come to my bed instead and have some fun.* Nowhere in the bible is this said, but books like that are meant to be studied and read between the lines.

Lilith is initially described as being the first woman for Adam in *The Alphabet of Ben Sira,* written between approximately 8-10th century CE:

"When God created Adam and saw that he was alone, He created a woman from dust, like him, and named her Lilith. But when God brought her to Adam, they immediately began to fight. Adam wanted her to lie beneath him, but Lilith insisted that he lie below her. When Lilith saw that they would never agree, she uttered God's Name and flew into the air and fled from Adam. Then Adam prayed to his Creator, saying, "Master of the Universe, the woman you gave me has already left me." So God called upon three angels, Senoy, Sansenoy, and Semangelof, to bring her back. God said, "Go and fetch Lilith. If she agrees to go back, fine. If not, bring her back by force."

The angels left at once and caught up with Lilith, who was living in a cave by the Red Sea, in the place where Pharaoh's army would drown. They seized her and said, "Your maker has commanded you to return to your husband at once. If you agree to come with us, fine; if not, we'll drown one hundred of your demonic offspring every day."

Lilith said, "Go ahead. But don't you know that I was created to strangle newborn infants, boys before the eighth day and girls before the twentieth? Let's make a deal. Whenever I see your names on an amulet, I will have no power over that infant." When the angels saw that was the best they would get from her, they agreed, so long as one hundred of her demon children perished every day.

That is why one hundred of Lilith's demon offspring perish daily, and that is why the names of the three angels are written on the amulets hung above the beds of newborn children. And when Lilith sees the names of the angels, she remembers her oath, and she leaves those children alone."

(Unknown, The Alphabet of Ben Sira, 8-10th Century CE)

There is a lot to unravel here. Lilith, much like Lucifer, sought equality and was stricken by Yahweh. Lilith didn't want to bow to Adam and let him ravage her, so she became demonic. Yahweh created her to give birth and for her children to be sacrificed. Yahweh tasked her to do the same to other mothers and their children. Lilith gets a bad reputation for being this baby-eating demon. Though, in actuality, *she* was the victim. She made deals with angels to save babies. As she was ordered to take innocents and have her own children slaughtered.

Along with the serpent, Lilith is also said to glamour in the form of an owl and a lion. All three of these animals are metaphysically known for specific traits. The owl represents wisdom and perception. The lion is strong and brave. The snake is stealthy and cunning.

Today, Lilith is worshipped as a Sumerian goddess, as those were her roots. She is welcomed in workings that involve sensuality, feminine strength, and intuition. Lilith is a goddess that will present you with trials to work with her. Because of her past, she doesn't easily trust. Having a bond with a goddess like Lilith is something that is sacred.

When working with her, show your vulnerability. Appear to ritual skyclad. Offer your essence, such as your blood or ejaculatory fluids. Lilith is big on personal connections. She requires a lot but also gives so much more in return. It's all about trust. Trust her, and she will teach you to trust yourself.

Here are some offering ideas for Lilith. You may notice how I've noted some of these items as baneful. Do not ingest these items in any form. You also shouldn't ingest rocks. Just a suggestion.

Poppies (Baneful)
White roses
Apple
Pomegranate
Red jewelry and clothing
Mugwort
Lily of the Valley (Baneful)
Mandrake (Baneful)
Azurite
Turquoise

Gen Z has recently been mocked for popularizing Lilith in a technique they coin as 'Siren Gaze,' with many of those practicing claiming to take inspiration from Lilith. The intent of these people on TikTok is actually to produce a glamour! Critics from the media are laughing at them, misinterpreting their work. The Daily Mail has an article titled: *Gen Z is mocked for claiming to invent SMILING: Bizarre new TikTok trend sees thousands raise their eyebrows and turn up their mouth to 'inspire obsession' from men.*

It's a shame that these neo-witches are being mocked for their trend, and I'm willing to bet most of them don't know how much truth there is in their techniques. It really doesn't get any more glamourous than this.

Influencers are teaching their followers how to smile with their eyes. How to draw energy from the power of suggestion. How to seduce an interest and inspire lust in others. They say they are embracing dark femininity and embodying goddesses like Lilith, luring men like the sirens did Odysseus's men. I couldn't be prouder.

The following sonnet and painting duo were an ode to the concept of femme fatale, women who use seduction to cause uproar with intent to get what they desire. Featured in the painting are poppies and white roses. The poem, originally titled *Lilith*, was later changed to *Body's Beauty*. Dante Gabriel Rossetti created both the poem and the famous oil painting. The poem is about going against the social norm and what it is to be a woman outside of the obedient housewife persona.

Body's Beauty
(Published 1868 in Swinburne's pamphlet review, *Notes on the Royal Academy Exhibition*)

"Of Adam's first wife, Lilith, it is told
(The witch he loved before the gift of Eve)
That, ere the snake's, her sweet tongue could deceive,
And her enchanted hair was the first gold.

And still she sits, young while the earth is old,
And, subtly of herself contemplative,
Draws men to watch the bright web she can
weave,
Till heart and body and life are in its hold.
The rose and poppy are her flower; for where
Is he not found, O Lilith, whom shed scent
And soft-shed kisses and soft sleep shall snare?
Lo! as that youth's eyes burned at thine, so went
Thy spell through him, and left his straight neck
bent
And round his heart one strangling golden hair."

(Rossetti, Body's Beauty, 1868)

(Rossetti, Lady Lilith)

Freya

Freya is a powerful Nordic goddess of love and war, two polarities many of us struggle with internally on a daily basis. We often go to war with ourselves with thoughts that we aren't good enough, aren't strong enough, and aren't prepared for the days that lie ahead. Freya is a goddess who is not afraid to be blunt. She can command an army with just a gaze. She is an embodiment of a powerful glamour.

She dons a cloak of hawk feathers, a symbol of her glamour. Like the owl, the hawk is symbolic of intelligence. They are messengers. Most importantly, they are leaders. Call upon Freya if you seek a leadership position in your life.

Another one of her familiars is a cat, as she is often depicted riding a chariot lead by a feline. Cats are known for their cunning and dexterity. If you are masking and looking to use a discrete glamour, Freya is a wonderful choice to work with. Her prowess and experience as a warrior goddess make her an excellent deity to work with for masking.

Here are some suggested offerings for Freya:

Honey
Chocolate
Mead
Bread
Falcon or hawk feathers
Jade

Amber
Emerald
Beads
Copper

Add feathers to your rite if you are trying to glamour your sex life. It is said that Freya provided her feathered cloak to those in need to spice things up. So, when you call to Freya, offer her some feathers in exchange to borrow that cloak.

Here is a glamour spell from my personal grimoire in which I choose Freya to work with. I know I said to attract energy, not people, but sometimes love is greater than sense. Once we have that special something, we don't want to lose it. Like Freya on the battlefield rooting for soldiers, I use that same energy to root for love.

Freya's Goddess Cloak

If your partner's eyes have a habit of wandering and trust is thin, try this chant with Freya. You will for sure command your lover's attention back.

"Fierce Freya, lend me your cloak
In tears, love, and blood, I soak
Keep his eyes on me
And my third eye on him
For others, he sees
He'll instantly go limp

Make me irresistible
May my scent drive him mad
Taurus, power of the bull
Show me I am wanted

May he treat me as his goddess
May he quiver in my presence

Let him shower me in affection
With lavish lust and perfect trust
May I hold all of his attention
May he only have good intentions

I want his heart, so mote it be

We'll never part, he's part of me"

The Morrigan

Another great goddess of war who uses glamour is the Morrigan. Like many other deities, this Celtic goddess embodies multiple phases and forms. The most common glamour she possesses is the ability to take the form of a raven. The raven form symbolizes that she is a messenger.

That is how we get the superstition of a crow crossing one's path being an omen. It is often associated with a loved one or yourself facing the reaper. However, it can be so much more. It is simply a warning to 'watch out.' Our goddess, our Phantom Queen, is not Death. She is a protector.

Other than appearing as a messenger in battles, she is also known to take on the form of a beautiful maiden, (Badb) a mother-like figure (Macha) and an old crone. (Namain) The Morrigan is one of many that is referred to as a triple goddess. These forms don't change the substance of our goddess; these are merely glamours.

Can you think of any other deity that the word 'the' precedes their name? How badass do you have to be to have your name spoken as a presentation?

That's the Morrigan. How we speak her name is another form of glamour. By saying it this way, we are manipulating our surroundings. Her name alone has the ability to command attention.

Here are some offering ideas for the Morrigan:

Yew
Red meat
Milk
Amethyst
Triquetra inscription
Black feathers
Clove oil
Dragon's blood
Thyme
Mugwort
Willow

Here is one of my personal glamour spells for the Morrigan. Use this glamour when you are about to go to a job interview.

The Morrigan Path to Success Glamour

Supplies:
Eyeliner and/or mascara
Mirror
Yellow candle
Thyme
Clove (Oil)

Instruction:
Gather your chosen makeup and place it in your sacred space. I recommend eyeliner and mascara

123

to symbolize boldness. I would stay away from intense colors, including eye shadows and lipsticks, since that could cause distraction. We want to draw attention to our eyes, and command attention, as the Morrigan would when serving/appearing as the maiden.

Either use a ritual dagger to inscribe a triquetra at the base of your candle or use chalk to draw one on the surface it's on. Dress the candle with thyme and clove. These herbs can be easily found in most spice cabinets. You don't need herbs that were especially cut for ritual purposes. You might even have clove oil in your medicine cupboard as it has a great use for toothaches. Light the candle and bless your makeup with the following chant.

Let the candle burn through and do not blow it out when you are finished. As it burns out, this is when you apply the makeup. Imagine applying your eyeliner like it's your war paint. Get ready for battle.

Chant:

"My eyes will line my path to success
As does how I look and how I dress

Bless this makeup so it may mask
The failures of my past

To have confidence is all I ask
Like the Morrigan on warpath

And like the raven, I will soar

A messenger you can't ignore

They need me and they will see
Warning from the Banshee Queen"

The Celts have an enriching history on beauty and hygiene. Having luxurious skin and long hair was a symbol of mystique and power. It was common to take extra care of your hair using beads, braids and ornaments. You know the cool Celtic knotwork you see in paintings? Celtic women braided their hair into that knotwork.

Did you know the Celts also invented soap? Thank the gods for the Celts! I'll put a recipe below on how to craft your own herbal soap to use for ritual baths or any type of daily cleansing. You can make your own glycerin soap base, but for ease of use, it's perfectly fine to buy it already made.

DIY Glamour Soap

Ingredients:
4oz cubed glycerin
1 orange
Rose petals
Jasmine petals
3 drops rose oil
1 tsp glitter

Supplies:
A gelatin mold or muffin tin
Eyedropper
Double boiler or microwave
Non-stick spray or oil

Instruction:
Take your orange and grate the zest. Place it in a
small bowl and set it aside. Take your glycerin
cubes and either melt them down in a double
boiler or simply put them in a microwave-safe
bowl. This works best on the stovetop, so you have
plenty of time to stir in your ingredients on low
heat once melted. After melting down, fold in your
desired amount of rose and jasmine petals into the
mix. Then pour in your dish of orange zest. Add in
rose oil. For fun, you may also add red or gold
glitter of your choice.

Once the concoction is mixed thoroughly, pick out
your favorite gelatin mold or muffin tin and spray it
down with nonstick spray or coat with
coconut/avocado oil. Pour the mixture into the
mold. I like to use heart-shaped molds from the
clearance rack after Valentine's Day. Pop the
molds into the freezer for two hours or put them in
the fridge overnight for the soap to harden.

And that's it! You now have homemade soap for
your glamour spells. While you can use this soap
for anything or for a base on any glamour spell, you
can also incorporate your craftwork in the cooking

process. As you stir the contents of your soap, try the following chant:

Chant:

"I enchant this soap with beauty
A conduit for a romance trope
Cleanse me in Aphrodite's Sea
Her glamour, I invoke"

Cerridwen

Another glamourous Celtic goddess is Cerridwen. Cerridwen is known for her sympathetic magick, using her cauldron to scry and to create her concoctions. Similar to mirrors, looking into a water-filled cauldron is a viable substitute in any glamour spell. She can also be called on when preparing water for ritual baths, infusing tea, and cooking.

Her cauldron represents prophecy and transformation. In her stories, she transforms into many things such as a hen, a greyhound, an otter, a hawk, and white sow.

In *The Mabinogion,* Cerridwen brews a potion to gift infinite knowledge to her son. The potion steeped for one year and a day. During this time, she employed a young man named Gwion to tend to the potion. And when stirring, three measly drops splashed onto his hand. Thus, Gwion retained the power of knowledge from the potion.

Cerridwen was devastated that the potion she had worked so hard on had been used on the wrong person. Even if an accident, Cerridwen was angry and accused Gwion of stealing it out of jealousy. She then sought to kill him, though the potion had also gifted Gwion Cerridwen's power of transformation.

"And she went forth after him, running. And he saw her and changed himself into a hare and fled. But she changed herself into a greyhound and turned him. And he ran towards a river and became a fish. And she, in the form of an otter-bitch, chased him under the water, until he was fain to turn himself into a bird of the air. She, as a hawk, followed him and gave him no rest in the sky. And just as she was about to stoop upon him, and he was in fear of death, he espied a heap of winnowed wheat on the floor of a barn, and he dropped among the wheat, and turned himself into one of the grains. Then she transformed herself into a high-crested black hen and went to the wheat and scratched it with her feet, and found him out and swallowed him." (Guest, 1877)

The gods across numerous mythos have always had interesting creation myths and unique tales of pregnancy and birth. This tale is no exception. When Cerridwen ate the grain that Gwion had transformed into, that 'seed' allowed Gwion to be reborn. Nine months later, Cerridwen gave birth to the son she didn't want and cast him away into the water within a leather satchel. She couldn't bear to murder him. After that, he was found and adopted. Gwion was reborn as Taliesin and grew up to be a handsome bard.

Here are some ideas of what you can offer Cerridwen:

Wheat
Cornbread
White silk
Chicken foot, feathers, or heart
Hawk feathers
Poetry

Whenever you cast a glamour in which you intend to change your appearance, ask Cerridwen for guidance. She responds best through water divination and likes to take part in brews. I'm not going to give you a potion recipe that you need to stir for a year and a day. We'll make an instant version.

Use this recipe when you are trying to make major transformations in your life. Modify the chant depending on what those changes are.

Cerridwen Cauldron Spell

Supplies:
Cauldron (or pot)
Mortar and pestle
Acorns

Hawthorn woodchips or bark (Can substitute
berries)
Lilac (Can substitute heliotrope)
Apple (Chopped)
Water

Instruction:
Grind the above ingredients with the mortar and
pestle, crushing the flowers, acorns, and mixing it
all together. Add a few drops of water to the
mixture for better consistency. Set this to the side
and heat your cauldron with water until boiling.
Either scoop the mixture raw and put it into the pot
directly, to strain later with cheesecloth, or let
steep in a tea ball and save any excess material for
another time.

Next, stir the mixture clockwise nine times and
chant to manifest your intended change. Below is
an example of a chant to transform physical
qualities. When you are done chanting, let the
brew cool and store in a container to keep in your
bathroom. The next time you take a bath or
shower, use this potion as a wash. With your
excess, give it as an offering to Cerridwen for your
gratitude.

Chant:

"I call thee, Cerridwen
To share thy thoughts
As I stir my mixing pot

Allow me to be born again
May this potion give me grace

May it help me lose the weight

Bless me with the fountain of your glamour
So that I may too, enamor"

Shichi-Fuku-Jin

The next deity actually embodies seven different
gods. Shichi-Fuku-Jin is the name given to the
seven Japanese gods of fortune. They are called
upon in any situation that demands luck or money.
They represent abundance and are summoned to
fight when all odds seem to be working against
you. With glamour, another energy you can
manipulate is chance. In numerology, seven is a
number of good luck.

The seven gods started being grouped together in
the early 1400's and since have rarely been
referred to as separate entities. They represent the
virtues of longevity, fortune, popularity, sincerity,
kindness, dignity, and magnanimity. Their names
are Ebisu, Daikoku, Benten, Bishamon, Fukurokuju,
Jurojin, and Hotei.

Ebisu is a god of professions that involve cultivation
and fishing specifically. Daikoku is the leader of the
seven deities and represents wealth, prosperity,
and abundance. Benten is a goddess of love and
divine femininity. Bishamon is a god of victories
and is a warrior. Fukurokuju is the god of wisdom
and longevity. And lastly, Hotei represents charity.

Traditionally, the Shichi-Fuku-Jin are celebrated on New Year's Eve when it is legend that the deities travel on their treasure ship and bestow gifts on those lucky enough to cross their path.

(Utamaro)

Gifts that were rumored to be given by the Shichi-Fuku-Jin include copper coins, jewels and gold coins, and along with obscure items like a key to the gods' storehouse, a hat that turns the wearer invisible, and a raincoat that protects the wearer from evil spirits.

Here are some offering suggestions to the Shichi-Fuku-Jin:

Coins
Sake
Jewelry
Copper
Gold
Rice
Fish

New Year's Eve Luck Spell

Supplies:
Mason jar
A handful of pennies or various coins
A shot of sake
1 tbsp rice
1 gold or yellow chime or taper candle
A petition slip and pen

Instruction:
Try to do this spell just before midnight on New Year's Eve. Take your mason jar and fill it with your coins, rice, and sake. Next, take your petition slip and write down some New Year's resolutions. Write down goals that you whole-heartedly intend on putting effort into achieving. Then fold the paper and add it to the jar. Seal the lid and give it a good shake, meditating on your goals becoming reality.

Next, we invoke the Shichi-Fuku-Jin. Light your candle and burn it on top of the jar. Let the wax drip from the tip of the candle until there is enough to seal the base onto the lid. Be sure to monitor the candle while it is lit until all the wax has melted.

It will drip over the lid and down the jar, sealing your spell.

After the candle is lit and burning, say the following invocation, also found in my *Book of Invocations*.

Chant:

"I call upon prosperity
Fortune and luck
I call upon bravery
May I be struck

With love and wealth
And perfect health

Abundance
A cup that never empties
Guidance
A purpose and expertise

Shichi-Fuku-Jin
Here and now, I invite you in
And I vow, to praise the seven

Nana, Hyo! Nana, Hyo!
Yumi O! Yumi O!
Shichi-Sama
Hear me, ima!

Shichi-Fuku-Jin
The seven wonders
I pray that you bring
Wisdom and answers"

At the end of the day, *you* are your higher power. Indulging in glamour teaches us to find solutions and happiness within ourselves. In magick, we look to the divine as well as internal and external factors. In glamour, we really put an emphasis on becoming a figural god or goddess. In a sense, it's okay to worship yourself. Praise yourself for a job well done. Accept rewards and compliments. These deities may help you find your inner goddess, but I promise that it's been there all along.

The Dreamscape

Another way to glamour is to do so in a subconscious or unconscious state. Dreams have been studied for as long as they've been misunderstood. Witches like to utilize dreams for psychic awareness and interpret them as they would prophetic visions.

We usually can't control when we receive messages in our dreams. We can only let the universe know that we're open to them. However, that doesn't limit you from creating your own messages and inserting them into the dreamscape.

The dreamscape is a canvas we can use to manifest our desires in the conscious mind. We can alter our own dreamscape or visit someone else's. The best way to use glamour in the dreamscape is to do so by lucid dreaming.

Before we get into the 'How-To', let's discuss the 'What.' What is lucid dreaming?

Lucid dreaming is when your mind is aware that it's in a dream. Although you are unconscious, your mind still has conscious awareness. When you are lucid, you have the ability to change how your dreamscape looks and functions.

Below, we will discuss methods produced by researchers and psychologists for enabling lucid dreams. We need to know the scientific methods before we can add our witchy twists. The first psychologist we will study is Stephen LaBerge.

Stephen coined the WILD method of lucid dreaming. WILD stands for Wake-Initiated Lucid Dream. The goal of this technique is to experience a hypnagogic hallucination. This is most easily done by setting an alarm to sound in the middle of your sleep, after you've already been in REM for an hour or so.

You will still be tired, but conscious. Your goal is to only stay awake for a few minutes. Then you resume your state of dreaming. You need to lie completely still. Your mind is trying to pull you back in the dreamscape, and you are resisting. You may hallucinate voices and images in your head as you resist, but you will remain conscious.

You may undergo sleep paralysis in this process. That might usually be a scary thing, but you are initiating it. It's safe here. If you have stress or worry in this state, you lose control. You *must* stay in control. This is key.

Your body may start to go numb. You feel like you can't move. Just sit back and relax. You're just waiting to enter the dreamscape. If this technique works, you usually end up in a place that resembles reality. You are probably in your bed. In your room. Ready to cause some dreamscape mischief.

Another one of LaBerge's methods is called MILD. What can I say? The man liked his acronyms. It stands for the Mnemonic Induction of Lucid Dreams. This technique is based on prospective memory. Prospective memories are just the reminders we give ourselves to complete tasks at a later time. It's the procrastination in us.

It can be things like remembering to take the trash to the curb, remembering to pay a bill or not forgetting your boyfriend's birthday. But we also use it in lucid dreaming. All you need to do to start is think of the last dream you remember.

Try to recall one part of the dream that defies reality. A common example is the ability to fly. We call these abilities dreamsigns, or sure signs that we're dreaming. Now, think about being back in the dream. Imagine the scenery, what you felt like, what you looked like. Tell yourself that you can only fly in your dreams. Then tell yourself that the next time you dream, you will remember your dream.

The next method we will look at is not my favorite. It's called reality checking. This method assumes that you may have issues distinguishing reality from a dream. Or, if you don't have that issue, it imposes that on you. The premise is metacognition. The more you train your brain during your conscious hours, the more likely you are to retain those habits in your dreams.

In this method, you literally can pinch yourself to see if you're dreaming. Even if you know you're not. When we're in a dream, it can seem vivid and very real. That's why we need to form habits while we're awake.

Set alarms on your phone to check. Monitor clocks and time. Time shifts differently in dreams, and you'd easily be able to differentiate a dream from reality. Look in a mirror. Our mind can't easily conceptualize mirror images in dreams.

When I choose to lucid dream, I meditate while laying down in bed. I imagine myself and create my dreamscape while I'm conscious. To do this, you have to be free from distraction and completely relaxed.

Now that we know how to initiate a lucid dream, we can talk about how to infuse them with glamour. The best way to use a glamour in a lucid dream is to re-enact a real-life scenario in the dreamscape. You are going to write the script. You play the main character. You decide the ending. Performing a glamour in the dreamscape will allow you to manifest in your conscious state.

First, let's add our witchy twists to the lucid processes. To start, I always tuck an amethyst under my pillow before initiating a lucid dream. Amethyst has a lot of uses, but its best use is for drawing out your psychic power. Opening your third eye. Prophetic dreams. Spiritual control. That makes it a perfect tool for our dreamscape glamour.

Another must preceding a dreamscape glamour is a cup of hot tea. Match your herbal choices to your intentions. Are you trying to win a contest? Catch the eyes of a love interest? Get a record deal?

Make your favorite herbal blend, add some flare, and the most important ingredient: Mugwort.

Mugwort is great for insomnia, menstrual cramps, and relieving stress. Its metaphysical properties include aiding witches in psychic and lucid dreaming. Although I must caution you to be careful, as mugwort can be baneful if ingested in large amounts. However, the amount you would use in tea is perfectly safe. People used to use mugwort in large quantities as a psychedelic ingredient since it had the ability to cause hallucination.

Ever wonder where the myth came from that witches could fly? The truth is, witches were *high*. Mugwort was a common ingredient in flying ointment that witches would put on the bottom of their feet to induce hallucination. To go to another realm. To be in a higher state of being. Don't try that at home. Stick to tea bags.

As you prepare to enter the dreamscape, you must again create a safe and sacred place while your body rests. Likely, you'll be cleansing the bed. You can burn mugwort like sage for this, or you can waft whatever herbs of protection you wish.

This step is important. Doing spellwork in the subconscious or unconscious state of mind can be dangerous. You want to make sure you don't attach to any malicious energies and that your physical body is a safe place to pop your spirit back into when your ritual has been completed.

As you're wafting your mugwort and sage around the bed, come up with a chant that ensures your safe journey and safe return. Also, be sure to state your intent for altering the dreamscape and what you would like to manifest. Here's an example chant to get you started. I chose to call on Hypnos, the Greek god of dreams, but you may call to whomever you like, if any deity at all. Calling on deities is never required.

Realm Travel Safety

Chant:

"Bless my bed, which tonight is my altar
I wish to alter the perception of _____ (Name or situation)
Hypnos, please accept my offer
Of mugwort, sage, and moonwater"

Before you lay down, bless yourself with moonwater. I trace a pentacle on my forehead when blessing myself. Your amethyst should already be under your pillow, and your tea nursed. The TV should have been shut off an hour ago, and the kids put to bed. Now it's just you and your dreamscape to paint. Before delving into a hypnagogic state, I like to balance my chakras and meditate. But that isn't necessary.

Once in your dreamscape, you need to manifest the setting and people you want to manipulate. If you are in your bedroom in your lucid dream, do a quick reality check to make sure you're actually in the dream. Then travel to your destination like you would as your conscious self. Don't try to stretch the rubber band too far in the dreamscape or do something that cannot be explained.

We don't want the dreamscape to collapse before we do our glamour. After your glamour is finished, you can fly, shoot lasers from your eyes, and turn the sun into an ice-cream sundae. Go wild! Let's talk about scenarios you may have for glamouring in a dreamscape.

First, imagine that your beloved cat, Scruffy, has run away. Very sad. But that's alright. Because through the dreamscape, you're going to find Scruffy. As long as you will it, it will happen. You not only control your actions in the dreamscape, but you also control the setting and those around you.

You wake up in your bedroom in the dreamscape. No Scruffy. You go to the kitchen to re-fill his food and water bowl. As you do so, imagine scratches at the door. You hear meowing. You go to the back door in a hurry and throw it open. Scruffy's floofy gray tail is straight up as he does a figure-eight around your legs in joy. You pick him up and hold him like it's been years.

Manifesting glamour through dreams isn't immediate. It could take a few days or so. There are a few rules, as well. Firstly, you can't make up people. If you will a person into your dreamscape, they must exist. If someone shows up that you don't know and you didn't create that person in your imagination, it's possibly someone who will impact your life in the future.

Dream Hopping

What makes lucid dreaming so powerful in any type of magick is the ability to enter someone else's dreamscape. Yes, you can manipulate someone else's dreams. The person may not remember it the next day, but you can subliminally influence them.

To do this, you must have a personal effect from that person. It doesn't have to be 'from' them like blood or hair. It can be a piece of clothing, a possession, or even a photo. It just has to be something you can hold onto or keep under your pillow. Prepare this object before you make your mugwort tea and settle down.

The object dedicated to the person needs to be spelled over an altar or sacred space before going into the dreamscape. There's no special setup or words required; you just need to state your intent with however you usually set up your spells. Before blessing the bed, simply do a simple chant for the object. I usually throw in a balance chant first, then light a candle with the person's name carved into the base. Use a white or purple candle if you choose this route.

Chant:

"May this (object) be the key
For walking into (Person's name) dream
As I keep this by my side
May my spirit be with them tonight

I wish no harm to (Person's name)
But for them to be under my charm
They shall wake up unalarmed
Once my glamour's been performed"

Some examples of why you would glamour someone via dream are to influence an employer for a raise, strengthen a friendship, will someone to tell the truth, heal an illness, and so much more. The possibilities are endless. Glamour works well in dreams because it's based on illusion and influence. Illusions are much easier to create in a dream.

Just like you can glamour a person, you can even glamour a place, for example, a garden. It's all about the shift in energy. Do you have a black thumb? The dreamscape is a good place to learn from your plants and influence them to grow for you. You can glamour bad energy from your home in the dreamscape if good 'ol sage cleansing isn't doing the trick. This is a lot safer than the astral projection alternative, since you are manifesting the dreamscape yourself rather than hopping realms.

I Can't Believe it's Not Glamour

If you ever feel that you are stuck in a glamour and not feeling yourself, try keeping daffodils around. These beautiful spring-blooming flowers are part of the genus, narcissus. If you aren't familiar with how the word narcissus came to be in a psychological sense, it's derived from a legend from Greek mythology.

Narkissos (Narcissus) was the local hottie in Thespaia. He hailed from a river spirit, Kephsos and a water nymph, Liriope. Narkissos was a picky guy. He had many suiters lined up for a chance at love, and he gave no one a chance. He rejected everyone that sought him with laughter and cruel jokes. The first girl who decided to shoot her shot was Ekho. Ekho was cursed by Hera to only be able to speak the words said before her. She could never speak her own mind and instead was stuck in an endless cycle of repetition. Poor Ekho could only haunt herself with the cruel words of Narkissos's rejection.

The next admirer was Ameinas, a young boy who also was harshly rejected by Narkissos. Ameinas was so engulfed by the pain of rejection that he soon took his own life at the feet of his crush. In his final moments, he invoked Nemesis to cast judgement on Narkissos and his cruel ways. Nemesis had witnessed the suffering done at the hands of Narkissos and answered Ameinas's prayer with haste, casting a spell on Narkissos to fall in love with his own reflection in the water before him. (Atsma, n.d.)

He could not pull his gaze away. Narkissos was infatuated with himself. He stayed rooted in the cave in which he resided, and nothing could pull him away. Some playful nymphs wanted to avenge their friends who were hurt by Narkissos, so they turned him into a narcissus flower.

(Fresco)

That's why we use daffodils to center ourselves again when we feel caught up in a glamour. Since these flowers are only readily available in the spring, keep a small bottle of narcissus essential oil to anoint yourself. There are also some nice oolong tea blends that contain narcissus as well, if you prefer.

Just remember that there is a thin line between confidence and conceitedness. Be sure you do not lose yourself in glamour. It can be addicting and intoxicating once you get the hang of it.

Perhaps recall a time when you hurt someone's feelings. Write about how you felt after and if your empathy could read their feelings.

NOTES

Mirror Cleanse

Another way you can re-ground yourself from a glamour high is to do a mirror cleanse. Use a wash as discussed in *Creating a Safe Space*. Or, make a solution of vinegar, water and if you have some, a few drops of narcissus essential oil. See below for instruction.

Supplies:
Mirror
Mirror wash (See above for ingredients)
Cloth
Lipstick

Instruction:

Use the mirror you usually cast glamours with and, if you use lipstick in your glamours, use one that has been enchanted specifically for this spell. Have your wash pre-made and ready in a dish on your altar.

Take your lipstick and write 'RELEASE' on the mirror. Hold the mirror up to your face and chant. After the chant, anoint the cloth with the wash and clean the mirror counterclockwise. This motion is symbolic to reversing the glamour.

Chant:

"I release myself from glamour
The constraints I bound myself
I realize that having more
Can be a curse rather a spell

As I wash away this mask
Free will is all I ask

Let me be me
So, mote it be"

Journal your feelings before bed and again the next
night. Do you feel more like yourself after this exercise?
Write about some things that are important to you.
Maybe jot down things that you usually like to do, that
you find no interest in lately.

NOTES

This next craft is a way to ground your glamours on the
go. It's a nice tool to relieve anxiety, stress, and

negative self-talk as well. You will either love or hate this tool solely because of its main ingredient.

Glitter Jar

Supplies:
Mason jar
Sharpie
2tbsp Glitter (Or however much fills your heart's content)
½ cup clear glue, liquid glycerin or corn syrup
Water
Hot glue
Silver candle

Instruction:
First, decide your intent for this jar. If it's just for grounding or getting back to the basics, use the sharpie to write 'balance' under the lid of the mason jar. This is also a good place to write positive affirmations. Just be sure to focus on one thing at a time.

Pick your glitter color based on the color correspondences we learned about earlier. For balance, use silver. Grey is symbolic of the 'in between' and is something I use often in my spells as a gray witch.

Start by adding ¼ cup of water to your mason jar. Then add in the glitter. Add in your thickening substance. I suggest using clear glue, corn syrup, or liquid glycerin, but you can get creative and experiment with others. Fill the rest of the jar up with water up to the fill line or about a half inch before full. You'll want to make sure the jar stays completely sealed so your glitter bomb doesn't escape, so use hot glue along the rim before sealing the jar.

For the candle magick portion of this spell, you can place the candle on top of the jar to have the melted wax pour down the sides, or you can just place it beside the jar on the altar. If putting the candle on top of the jar, make sure to light a match under the base to melt the hot wax onto the lid. Then quickly and firmly place the candle onto the jar so it doesn't move. You don't want your candle to tip over and burn your house down. Be safe about this and don't leave it unattended.

You only need to chant once to seal the spell. And whenever you want to manifest your intent, shake the jar and visualize. If you have a hard time visualizing, just lose yourself in the glitter. That's what it's there for. Keep this on your desk at work, at school, or in the center console of your car. Wherever you need to de-stress and ground yourself most.

Chant:

"I bind balance to this jar
A perfect blend of light and dark
Above, below, and in between
When I shake this jar, I will come clean"

Once glamour has gone sour or if your manipulation spell backfired, it's good to keep an evil eye talisman at hand. You've definitely seen this symbol before. It's a black pupil, with a light blue circle surrounding it, followed by a white circle and dark blue. Like you are able to use gaze to enamor allure, it can also be used to curse.

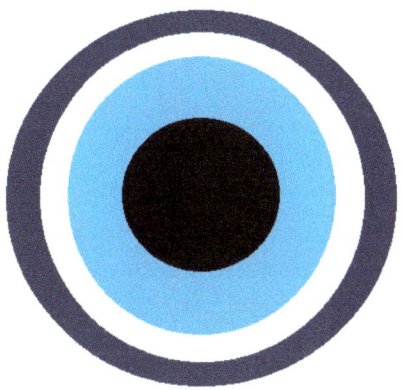

Wearing this symbol is a form of apotropaic magick, or reflective magick. The eye is symbolic of a mirror, the sun, the moon, a portal to spiritual awakening. When you are overwhelmed, you close your eyes and take a breath. At death, we close our eyes.

There is finality in this symbolism. When you 'turn a blind eye', you make something no longer your problem. It's as simple as that.

If someone you know has a less than glamourous attitude toward you, and you simply want to reflect that negative energy, here's a spell to do just that. We aren't cursing, merely returning an unwanted gift. Reflection spells are important to know if you practice manipulation magick. Because when you're battling someone else's gross energy, your magick only works if your willpower is greater than their desire to mess things up.

Evil Eye Reflection

Supplies:
$1 USD bill

Handheld mirror
White tea light candle
Salt

<u>Instruction</u>:
Take out a crisp one-dollar bill and turn it to the side
that has the eye of providence and the eagle. Set it on
top of your mirror upon your altar. Light the tea light
candle and place it above where you set the dollar bill.
Take your salt and sprinkle it in the shape of a
downward triangle around the mirror. The point should
be facing you.

Pick up the bill and hold it up. Fold the paper away from
you three times starting on the right side. Make sure to
fold the creases tight. You should just have the eye of
providence showing now, the pyramid with the eye
above it. Place it on the mirror. Replace the blank space
below with the person's name you are reflecting energy
toward.

<u>Chant</u>:

"I call to me the all-seeing eye
_____'s actions are not justified
For when those who live in vain

153

Get away with anything
They never feel the pain
The agony they fling

I reflect their energy
And all the harm they've done to me

I turn a blind eye
Take back the tears I've cried

The all-seeing eye
Is a mirror to the soul
So, whenever they gaze
Upon their face
They'll see a black hole"

Glamour with Greater Purpose

As we've covered, glamour not only affects ourselves but also has a direct influence on the people and energies around us. There is so much that can be done with glamour, especially on the macroscopic level, and that includes helping others. Macro magick.

In preparation for this glamour usage, we need to talk about empathy and mindfulness. When I was younger, I struggled to control my empathy. I am extremely sensitive to others and how they feel. I am an empath to the point of feeling other people's physical pain.

My mom has always had MS. It's a debilitating condition that affects your muscular and nervous system. Before she knew it was MS, I was about six years old. I remember my knees going weak and all of a sudden, my legs didn't work. Scared, I went crying to my mom. But I saw her crying as well.

I dried my tears and went over to her. She was clenching her legs and trembling. I didn't tell her what I was feeling, but I saw her fear. I became scared too. That was the first instance I felt empathy on a physical level. A week later, she went to a neurologist and got her diagnosis.

Empathy doesn't always have to be so intense. Some may never feel it on that spiritual level, and that's okay. We can pick up other people's feelings through their demeanor. Pay attention to their tone of voice, how loud or soft they speak. Do they stutter? Do they take large sighs and scrunch their face? Look at their brows, body language, and breathing patterns.

Some people have the gift of feeling or knowing and don't need to pay special attention to these signs. The intensity of empathy can be controlled toward a person or situation. You can turn it off, like a switch, and reflect energy back at people. Because empathy is not just a manifestation of feelings that you see; it's an energy that you feel.

Mindfulness pairs well with empathy. It's our ability to keep composure and balance through a variety of different situations. Basically, it's keeping a healthy mind and being aware of when it's unhealthy and you're out of balance. Aside from traditional meditations of balancing our chakras, mindful meditation is another way to achieve a similar goal.

Instead of working through imagery, we are working through thought. Mindful meditation is where we do our re-framing and control our empathy. It's letting go of judgement and pre-conceived notions. We are living life in the moment when we show mindfulness rather than worrying about things we have no control over.

Let go of what you cannot control and focus on things you can. Look for specific objects in the room and in your mind identify their shape, color, and usefulness. By focusing on facts, you are training your brain to be mindful.

Posture and position are important when it comes to mindful meditation. Sit up straight and don't slouch. We are more assertive with good posture. You should be in an active listening position. But instead of listening to someone else, we are going to listen to our mind and spirit.

Next, unclench your jaw. You'd be surprised how often throughout the day your teeth are clenched together in an unconscious stress response. Relax your face muscles. Now, breathe. Think about nothing but breathing. Inhale. Exhale. Inhale. Exhale. This is mindful meditation. Now that you are mindful, you can more easily tap into empathy and work with glamour with a greater purpose.

Helping Crossover

One way to use glamour to help others is the process of helping people pass over. Death is something we all have in common, and just the thought of our own demise can instill great fear. Glamour can be used to give those ready to cross peace of mind and comfort in their final moments.

Obviously, not everyone has the same beliefs. Your purpose here isn't to go on a mission and tell them about the arms of your goddess or about their next life as a badass through reincarnation. No. You need to tap into your empathy.

Help this person manifest their version of heaven. Call to angels. Allah. Yahweh. Transfer love and peace to them. In your head, repeat 'You are forgiven' like a mantra to soothe any regrets they have. Hold their hand and transfer your energy as one last adrenaline boost.

Even if this person leaving your world is completely soul-crushing to witness, you know it's right to tell them it's okay to go. They're suffering. You're suffering, in turn, by watching their pain at a distance.

This isn't permission to expedite someone's dying process. Don't wish for death if this person is still fighting. You'll know when someone is tired. You can tell when they're done fighting. All you need to do is provide acceptance. Give them your glamour.

The Beauty of Birth

Let's pivot to a more lighthearted subject. Life. Giving birth is a very special moment in a parent's life. During this time, we can use our glamour to bless the mother during her term, labor, and post-labor stages. And of course, we can also provide a glamour for the newborn.

For Moms-To-Be, it is important to read the section on *Creating a Safe Space*, since during your nine months of preparation, nesting is a huge part of your maternal process. Nesting is the mechanism every mother goes through to create a welcoming space for her baby. We get organized. We coordinate onesies by color and time of day. We research the best bottles and car seats. We do everything in our power to prepare for that day we get to meet our baby.

Whether you're a Mom-To-Be, or want to help one, there are glamours you can cast to help mothers stay sane. Inscribe words of power onto your candle, birch bark or other item that symbolizes the mother figure. Manifest words like patience, breathing, healthy, rest, grace, joy, and abundance.

Being a parent is hard work. While yes, pregnancy can be very exciting, it can also be extremely stressful. There is no shortage of things to worry about in this day and age. Can you financially support another mouth to feed? What about daycare if you have to work? You will lose sleep, feel physically ill, and your hormones will cause an emotional rift.

Here's a glamour spell with the intent to create an energy of peace and drowsiness. This is to help those with insomnia or those haunted by weird pregnancy nightmares.

Sandman Glamour

Use a blue candle and inscribe words of power at the base relating to good rest and health. Sprinkle a salt circle around the candle and put a pinch in a bowl of water to place next to the candle.

We are going to work with the goddess Diana. Her connection to the phases of the moon represents the journey of a woman. She protects mothers during pregnancy and childbirth. We will also work with Hypnos, the god of sleep.

Light the candle and chant:

"Diana

Matron goddess, I call to thee
May you witness my prayer for peace
By your power, this pregnancy thrives
By both the mother's and baby's lives

Diana, my mother witch
May she carry without hitch

Let Hypnos grant her rest
Great Mother, you know best

That good health comes to those refreshed
May ailments once she has slept
So, mote it be by the will of my breath"

Blow the candle out to seal the spell. At this, may the mother find good rest. And that's all there is to it.

You can perform glamours similarly throughout labor with breathing techniques. It's all about mind over matter. Keep repeating in your head your breathing cues. Your mantra should be something short. *I can do this. Keep going.*

You can also try glamours for the post-partum stage of pregnancy. Depression is bad enough; post-partum depression is a whole other league of emotions to untangle. While it affects everyone differently and some are lucky enough to not experience it at all, creating a place of glamour to make these transitions go smoothly is never a bad idea.

Stick with your self-encouragement and daily affirmations to yourself in the mirror through these difficult times. Remember how to love yourself. If you can't love yourself, you can't love anyone else. You can't take care of another life if you can't take care of yourself. I'll repeat it again: **Self-care isn't selfish.**

Bestowing glamour upon an infant is a much simpler concept. Think of the three faeries in Sleeping Beauty. Flora gives Aurora the gift of beauty, Fauna gives her the gift of song, and Merryweather provides the gift of uncrossing. Though again, this is fiction, it is an accurate example of how glamour can be used to bestow upon someone else.

All you need to do is bless a gift to the child, like clothing or a rattle. It has to be something they would use. Or, you can simply transfer energy by touch and manifest out loud the gift you are giving. At this time, I would also ask a god or goddess to protect the child at the parent's consent.

As we use glamours on ourselves to battle anxiety and depression, we can also cast glamours on other people to assist in their battles as well. Our friends will cry for help if they trust us. Rather than feeling helpless for them, try taking action.

I've had friends that were suicidal and long past their breaking point in which I've helped. Though, I've always done so in secret. Even in helping others, glamour still works best when blossomed from self-confidence. We want this loved one to think that they're the reason things are better.

And that's okay. We don't cast spells for thanks; we do it for our own satisfaction and enlightenment. And let's face it, having people mentally unwell around us, whom we care for, is also draining on our own spirit through empathy.

In a way, we are going to possess their spirit to help give our friend the boost they need. We are going to do those affirmations and work with a mirror again. However, the mirror magick is going to go a bit deeper. Mirrors are great tools for scrying. Any mirror can work, but if you have a black mirror available, use this one. Obsidian mirrors are gorgeous tools for scrying.

BFF Boost

Supplies:
Mirror
Black chime/votive/tealight candle
White chime/votive/tealight candle
Yellow pillar candle
Essential Oil (Bergamot, orange, or lemon are great choices)

Instruction:
As you would gaze into a crystal ball, do so in the mirror. Perform deep breathing exercises. As you breathe in, take in the energies around you. And with each breath out, release your intentions into being. With each exhale, your features start to change. You are morphing your mirrored image into the face of your friend. By doing this, you are projecting yourself onto them.

When you are completely in focus and you are scrying the Image of your friend, keep eye contact.

Use their facial expressions. Their mannerisms. Put your spirit on the bleachers for now, but keep your intent at the front of your mind.

The first chant for any spell like this is always the same for me. Balance is a huge part of my work, and doing something that messes with your balance and taking on energies that can affect your spirit must be cautioned.

The chant below is repeated thrice as you light both the white candle (as you call to your lighter half) and the black candle. (as you call to your darker half) This isn't a spell to decipher good and evil. It is simply to accept that there cannot be shadow without the light.

As you call upon the light energy, imagine a bright white orb in your hand. As you call upon the dark energy, imagine an obsidian-colored orb. The candle flames grow and falter for each side you call toward, respectively. At the end of the third time, repeating the chant, combining the orbs in the palms of your hand and releasing a deep breath.

First Chant:

"I call upon my lighter half
To aid me in this right-hand craft
May the balance not be broken
By these words that I have spoken
Awaken

I call upon my darker half
To aid me in this left-hand craft

May the balance not be broken
By these words that I have spoken
Awaken"

Further Instruction:
Now that you have found your balance, it's time to glamour your friend. Use your willpower to maintain their appearance as you scry into the mirror. It's time to dress the yellow pillar candle in oil and light it. Chant the following spell and affirmations, replacing '_____' with your friend's name.

When you are done, close your eyes to seal the spell and meditate for a moment. Do deep breathing exercises to get back into yourself and release from your friend's spirit. Come to slowly and open your eyes when done. Let the candles burn down.

Chant:

"I take on the form of _____, a person dear to me
I transform their way of thought
And help them see what I see

I am _____
I am beautiful
I am strong
I am deserving of love
I am _____

I am _____
I will get better
I am stronger than my pain

I have so much life to gain
I am _____

I am _____
I am happiness
I am light
I'm bigger than my demons
I am _____"

My intention with this book is to help manifest glamour into people's day-to-day lives. I hope you found this to be a useful tool in creating your own beauty through art and spirit. I hope you found beauty in yourself. We all come from different places and backgrounds, but we all use the same energy.

Anyone can have glamour in their lives, whether you're a witch or not. There is magick everywhere, and you make the choice whether to recognize it. When times are low, we take these magickal moments for granted. It's easy to see the bad when there are unexpected circumstances and challenges. Instead of expecting everything to crash and burn when things are difficult, try seeing these moments as trials of your deities or opportunities to shine.

There isn't one simple recipe to be 'okay.' But I can teach you how to thrive with what you have. When people think of glamour, I'm sure fancy outfits, makeup, and jewelry all come to mind. Maybe it's the CoverGirl magazine you used to worship. Maybe it's the popular girl in school that made you feel less than. But I can assure you, that's not what glamour is about.

While yes, glamour in a magickal sense is based on illusion and manipulation, the concept of what is glamourous is different for everyone. At the end of the day when you wind down for bed, I hope you turn off your glamour and look in the mirror, choosing to accept yourself. Because the demeanor you embodied for the day wasn't created. It was always inside of you. And by doing these crafts, you at some point probably realized this.

Sometimes, we just need a nudge in the right direction. You have the power to control how you perceive yourself. And if you have confidence, other people will see the same person. To an extent, magick casts a placebo effect. Eventually, you won't need the glamour spell to do these things, and it will come naturally. But to me, that's magick. That's beautiful.

Here I will include exercises for daily affirmations, additional recipes, and activities to influence your glamour. As always, feel free to modify these suggestions to fit them more personally into your life. Make notes on your thoughts throughout these exercises before and after you perform them. As previously suggested, it may be best to keep a separate journal from your general craftwork, but use this book as a place to get started. A marked-up book is a well-loved book. Now, go on and make it your own.

Exercise 1 – Morning Affirmations

Start by noting your thoughts first thing in the morning.

NOTES

Morning Mirror Affirmations

Find a mirror and look yourself in the eyes. Take a piece of tourmaline and clasp it as you say the following chant. Massage it with patchouli oil. Repeat this chant every day for seven days and keep the crystal on your person. Every time you feel doubt in one of these affirmations, grasp the crystal in your palm and absorb the power of the grounding energies you enchanted it with that morning.

Chant:

"Today is going to be a good day. I am strong. I am stable. I am grounded. Nothing will be given to me that I can't handle. I have beauty physically and spiritually. My guides will be with me today to remind me of this. I dedicate this tourmaline to them and infuse their borrowed power and the resilience of my own spirit within it. So, mote it be."

After seven days of doing this affirmation, I want you to note how you feel below. Give your guides and your crystal a break. Charge your tourmaline under the next new moon.

NOTES

Exercise 2 – Evening Affirmations

Start by noting your thoughts after you've settled down for the night and are getting ready for bed. Have you had trouble sleeping lately with insomnia and frequent waking? Nightmares? Anxiety? Write it down.

Find a piece of amethyst and massage it with lavender oil. This will be placed under your pillow after the following chant. Anytime you are having issues with sleep, re-charge the amethyst.

Chant:

"My dreams from now on will be guarded by Hypnos. It's time for Morpheus to have some rest. With this, my amethyst is blessed. May it lend me its peace in nightmare's duress. And when I wake, may I be at ease. May the breeze of the Night's wind touch my cheek, so I get a good night's sleep."

Note any dreams of interest below and how you interpret them. Write down any difficulties or patterns you've had in your sleep during this exercise.

NOTES

Tea Blends with Purpose

Use this section merely as a resource. I only provide examples of your options, but they are indeed limitless. If you do stray away from these recipes, just be sure the herbs you are using are safe to ingest. Even some that are deemed safe can be unsafe in certain amounts.

While these recipes can be done without actual tea leaves, I leave that to you. For proper digestion, use a base tea such as green tea, black tea, or white tea leaves.

Soothing Your Spirit

1 part jasmine flower
1 part chamomile

This tea is best served with honey, and for that I recommend one containing sage. Chamomile has long been a remedy for sickness in both physical and mental ailments. I personally have found that jasmine also has a use to soothe migraines.

Soft Skin

1 part marshmallow
1 part echinacea
1 part chamomile

Try adding cream or milk to this brew to amplify the effects. After drinking this tea weekly, you'll notice a difference in your complexion and improved softness of your skin. On top of skin health, this blend also kicks butt when it comes to infections. It's a shot of immune-boosters!

A Lasting Love

1 part hibiscus
1 part rose hips
1 part orange peel

This tea is best served with a sweetener such as sugar or stevia. Along with attracting others, you are sure to find satisfaction within yourself if you start your day out with this blend.

Attracting Money

1 part mint
1 part ginger

To sweeten this blend, try adding one drop of vanilla extract. Mint is a well-known herb to help soothe colds and congestion.

Appetite Suppressant

1 part ginger
1 part dandelion
1 part rosemary

Drink this blend raw for the best experience. No sweeteners, no nothing. It will give you a wake-up call and keep your hunger under control. Your extra dandelion in the summertime makes a tasty treat fried up, as well. (Just be light on the oil)

Curating Confidence

1 part elderberry
1 part blueberry (dried or frozen)
1 part blackberry leaves

This blend is surely a pick-me-up! As well as containing metaphysical properties to fight colds, this blend also keeps you calm, collected, and motivated. Use any sweetener for this tea, but it does possess a wonderful sweetness on its own from the blueberries.

Strengthening Your Third Eye

1 part lavender

1 part ginger
1 part star anise

While strengthening your psychic energies and your connection to the divine with this tea, you are also aiding your digestion and breathing. Lavender also assists with anxiety and depression.

Engaging with Empathy

1 part lavender
1 part fennel
2 hawthorn berries (Warning: Use the berries in tea only. You should not eat the berries whole because of potential side effects of the seeds)

This blend will awaken your senses and put your emotional radar on high alert. Add a squeeze of lemon for that extra 'oomph.' I prefer this one without any sweetener.

Acne Be Gone

1 part thyme
1 part lavender
1 part echinacea

So, magick is magick in all. But there are practical ways to change things about our body that we don't like. A daily dose of these herbs is a healthy way to decrease blemishes and acne. And it tastes delicious!

Come to Me Tea

1 part ginseng
1 part saw palmetto
1-part damiana leaf

This will spike your libido in no time. This works for any sexual activity when you want to create *the mood*. Sweeten with a teaspoon of honey for your honey.

Exercise 3 – Creating a Talisman

The following exercise takes influence from African-American folk magic. If you practice Hoodoo, this would be a variation of a mojo bag or gris-gris bag. Since I do not follow this path, I do not claim that the following is a recipe for gris-gris, but rather a personal talisman.

The point of these pouches is to have a spell on the go that you can meditate on for immediate relief. We don't always have the means or the time to do fancy rituals. Being in a public setting also makes a difference, since many of us choose our beliefs to be practiced privately.

The following talisman should be used to attract good luck. Start by taking notes on what good luck means to you, if you believe in it, or when you experienced luck.

Ancestor Talisman

To start, obtain a small piece of cloth or fabric.
Shape doesn't matter, as long as it's large enough
to be tied together in a satchel and small enough to
be concealed on your person, whether that be in
your pocket or on your keychain.

Lay out the fabric on your altar or sacred space. Next, light a candle to call to your spirits or deities of choice.

Because of this spell's influence having Hoodoo roots, I like to call to my ancestors. I also invoke my spirit guide. Try the following invocation to the ancestors, also found in my *Book of Invocations*:

Chant:

"I call to my bloodline
My sacred fire
With the aid of my shrine
May barrier shatter

Between then and now

What was and is
The time enow
It is my wish

I set libation
For your peace
And hope you'll listen
To my plea

Take form, beloved _____ (Specific name, or just
say 'ancestors')
Help is needed
From eyes of the dead

Travel Styx, Charon reverse
Take away the silence
Of Dead Man's Curse
And sleep immense

I prithee peace
I prithee well
Now release
From the spirit well"

Whenever you invoke your ancestors, be sure to
leave them an abundant treat or offering. They are
the reason you exist, and it's important to show
them respect.

There are plenty of plants and herbs that
correspond to bringing luck. However, I like to use
ginger, cinnamon, clove, and cardamom. First of all,
these scents smell divine. This combination
definitely makes me feel like I'm breathing in a hot
cup of chai tea and the winds of autumn. These

ingredients are all multi-purpose, but they all attract luck in a metaphysical sense.

Place your array of herbs onto the cloth and seal the spell as you tie it together with twine. Wear it on your person to attract luck, and when you feel your luck has turned, replace the herbs and make the talisman again.

As you tie the satchel, you are sealing the spell. As you do this, say the following chant.

Chant:

"Bless these herbs, so they may be a magnet for luck. Ginger, so that my actions do not hinder my options. Cinnamon to bring me money. Clove to make my circle grow. Cardamom to will luck to my palm. Ancestors, please guide me in my path. Spirit, see to it that I don't stray. And may luck find me today."

After a few days of wearing the talisman, note your experiences and coincidences. Write about your perception of luck now and things that have happened which you're grateful for.

NOTES

Dark Moon Talisman

This next talisman spell encourages new opportunities to come your way. Do this spell when you are in a repetitive cycle of feeling 'stuck.' Or even when you feel that you have lost your motivation and have nothing to fight for. The power of this talisman invites change into your life.

Supplies:
An old key

Black candle
String
Garlic
Eggshells
Paper plate
House dust, old incense, dead flowers, etc. (Do some house cleaning)

Instruction:

Perform this spell on the dark moon, preferably during Noumenia for three days. Traditionally in Hellenic Greece, the new moon was celebrated for three days, honoring Hekate and leaving her libation at the crossroads. The Deipnon is the third day of the new moon, just before it goes into waxing. The first two days are referred to as the Noumenia, followed by Agathos Daimon. Light a candle for Hekate each of the three days and give her one offering per day on your altar. Honey and cakes make good offerings. Next to the candle, leave the key. The key is a tool of Hekate, which is why we are calling to her.

On the last day, Deipnon, you sacrifice the most. Gather things like garlic cloves and eggshells and put them on a paper plate. I say use paper so it can be disposed of the next day. You don't want to take this stuff back inside. Traditionally, crossroads in Greece translated to someone's front porch. So that's where we throw our offerings during Deipnon. Along with our pungent gifts, also include leftover incense ash, dead flowers, house dust, and anything else 'unclean' or 'no good.' Since the dark moon is a time of change, this is the time to get the shit out of your life, so we can invite good changes after the rite.

It is very important that on the Deipnon, when you leave your offerings on the porch, turn around and don't look back. Shut the door behind you and don't go back outside until dawn. Legend says that Hekate comes with her hounds of death to collect the dead. If you catch their sight as she's making her rounds, her hounds may attack.

Before you bring your contents to the crossroads, tie the key around the string and put it around your neck like a necklace. Then say the following chant. On the next morning, dispose of anything left that was offered. Do NOT bring any part of the offering inside your house. Wear the key until the next Noumenia and then place it back on your altar.

Chant:

"Hekate, I call thee forth
To open up a new door

Give me opportunity
Show me greatness where I cannot see

As I carry 'round your key
I ask that you stay with me

And before the next Deipnon
To change, I will be drawn

And in thanks of your direction
I give my blessings and affection"

Exercise 4 – Manifesting Your Spirit Guide

The purpose of this glamour is to manifest the traits of your spirit guide through glamour magick. If you do not have a spirit guide, imagine the traits of your favorite animal or coordinated astrological symbol and the metaphysical traits they represent. For example, you can manifest the cunning of a serpent, the intelligence of the owl, the dexterity of a cat, or the stable root chakra of the bull.

My spirit guide is the sparrow. In deep meditation, I see him in animal form, human form, and a combination of the two.

The sparrow has many metaphysical associations. Like most birds, they represent wisdom and can appear as messengers to warn you of big life events. Sparrows also represent hard work ethic, teamwork, friendships, and minimalism. It's funny, because I struggle with all of these things sometimes, while at other times I thrive.

Before starting the spell, reflect on your spirit guide or chosen animal. How do they complement you?

Spirit Guide Evocation

I am going to give you an example of a glamour spell I use when working with my spirit guide, Mael. I recommend having a dedication to your spirit guide always present on your altar, or to give them a separate altar for themselves. My object of choice is an abandoned nest I found on my way back from outdoor meditation one day.

It was definitely a sign from Mael, since I had come into nature to reflect on why I hadn't been practicing for a while or giving time to my craft. So of course, I went back home and dedicated it to him as thanks. It's symbolic to show that he always has a place in my home.

For manifesting Mael into a glamour, I start out by setting out objects and associations on my altar that represent his qualities. Then, I position crystals like tourmaline, clear quartz, citrine, tiger's eye, fluorite and peridot. While the sparrow is mostly tied to the element of air, water comes in at a close second. I light an incense with a nice citrus scent and leave out a small dish of water. If I have any feathers recently collected, I add those as well. This is my chant.

Chant:

"Mael, I praise you as my shadow
For when in doubt, I know you'll follow

I ask for borrowed power
For your traits, I honor

Please lend me wisdom when I'm crossed
Please lend me friendship when I'm lost

Motivation when I'm drained
Appreciation when it rains

I spread my arms like feathers
May I embody these traits of yours
And when I'm doing better

I'll return them to you once more"

Of course, your personal chant to your guide will be much different than mine. This is just a guideline. If you want to call on your guide more generically, try using an invocation like this, also found in my *Book of Invocations*.

Chant:

"Spirit Guide
I call ye hence
I sing your name
Raise my defenses

_____ (Speak their name)

Praise be unto thee
Walk with me
The path of dreams
Of the unseen
Anomalies

_____ (Speak their name)

I invoke thee here and now
As long as thee allow"

How did it feel communicating with your guide? Did you notice a difference in your nature throughout the day? Write your feelings below.

NOTES

Humans, plants, and animals all possess spirit residue. Although sometimes stronger than others, this energy is exuded out into our surroundings and nature.

Examples are our tears that fall from our face, our laughter that breaks the silence and screams cutting through the air. Energy can neither be created nor destroyed. Only changed. And there are many tools of nature that don't always come to mind when performing magick.

Just because a spirit isn't your guide doesn't mean you can't ask for guidance. This section will go through items you can find in nature that hold spirit residue which can be used in practical spellwork.

I suggest you gather these items ethically as you stumble upon them in nature. Do not disturb any living creature or their den.

But like energy, nature shifts. Birds leave their nests. Bucks shed their antlers. There are plenty of ways to ethically source nature's raw ingredients to obtain spiritual residue for your glamour spells. When in doubt, ask your personal spirit guide to help you connect with nature and ask permission.

And whenever you go on a nature hike, bring a backpack, gloves, jars, and satchels. You never know what you'll find while scavenging, and it's best to be prepared. If you happen across something in nature that has crossed over and you wish to scavenge for bones and remains, always handle it with caution and gloves. Other scavengers and the process of decay leave animals prone to disease. Below is a list of nature's goodies, their symbolism, and uses.

Items with Spiritual Residue

Snakeskin: Snakes represent many of the goddesses worshipped today. They get a bad reputation for being 'evil', but that couldn't be further from the truth. Any animal that sheds their skin is symbolic of transformation.

The symbol of the ouroboros represents the circle of life and the cycles of eternity, and in some cultures, the snake also represents immortality. They represent the underworld and spiritual journeys. When you feel stuck at a crossroads, if you are sick, in need of change, or in general want to add potency to your spellwork, snakeskin is a great find in nature.

Eggshells: Eggshells are commonly used in fertility spells and those involving rebirth of any kind. This could be literal or figurative. Birth and death are the two absolutes in nature. The shells can be ground into a fine powder with a mortar and pestle and combined with loose incense during a glamour for positive transformation. If you have a tarot deck, pull the death card and meditate with it as the incense burns.

Feathers: Feathers are symbolic of transformation and the element air. Use feathers in your glamour for any spell that you are using to transform yourself for the better. Another use for feathers is for when you or a loved one feels they are trapped in a situation, whether that be in the form of a partner, a parent, or legal matters. Place a feather under your pillow and work your glamour in the dreamscape to solve these issues. Birds also represent messengers, and the dreamscape is a good place to start to be open to receiving those messages.

Honeycomb: Honeycomb is generally used in glamour spells for sweetening. By sweetening, I mean love and envy spells. Use honey as a binder in any type of glamour, add it to tea, or use it in a jar spell.

Anthill dust: Creepy crawlies aren't something most witches use in their spellwork, but this is something you may wish to reconsider. The dedication and work ethic of an ant colony to their queen is unmatched. Use anthill dust in glamours where you want to incite determination and work ethic. You may also wish to use it when you are adamant about achieving your goals and as symbolism of forging your own path. This also makes a great addition to a goofer dust recipe.

Bones: There are so many uses for bones in witchcraft, especially glamour. Use bones in any glamour that involves liminal magick. If you are helping someone transition to the end of their cycle, welcoming a new life, or enlisting help from a spirit that has passed, bones are a great use. They can be ground in powder and added to incense or goofer dust. They can be tossed as an oracle for scrying. And depending on the type of glamour you want to achieve, this will affect which bones you should consider for your rite. For getting in someone's head, you may use a skull. For sex magick, you may use a phallic bone.

Teeth: Showing teeth is a sign of aggression and warning. Use teeth in a glamour where the intent is for someone to back off. Prime examples are nosy neighbors, gossipers, or micromanagers.

Antlers/Horns: There are many masculine deities represented by antlers and horns, such as Pan and Cernunnos. Use antlers or horns in a glamour in which you are trying to assert dominance, primitive magick, or in sex magick.

Chrysalis/Cocoon: Like the feather, a chrysalis or cocoon are tools or transformation. It's common to stumble upon a burst shell of a former caterpillar on a hike in the woods. Next time you see one, gently transfer it into a satchel or jar to use in your next glamour. They are versatile for almost any glamour spell.

Dog hair: If you don't have a dog, no worries, I have an abundance of dog hair at my house. After just a day's worth of sweeping, I have enough to construct a whole new dog. Dogs are known for their loyalty. Use dog hair in a spell where someone has been disloyal to you, and you want to change that.

Whiskers: Whiskers are like antennas for animals. They add an extra layer of sensory to help them as either predator or prey. Use whiskers in a glamour where scrying is necessary. They will aid your psychic awareness and increase your sensory perceptions.

Here is a glamour for attracting attention, utilizing a peacock's feather. When foraging and scavenging for such items in nature, be sure to give thanks to the spirit of the forest and the plant or animal that the offering came from. A quick prayer will suffice, but some people also provide biodegradable offerings in return.

Eyes on Me

Supplies:
Peacock Feather
Himalayan Pink Salt
Scissors
Licorice Root

Orris Root
Matches
Flameproof Dish
Rum

Instruction:

Prepare your flameproof dish on your altar. I use my mortar for spells that involve small fires. Alternatively, you can burn in a fireplace or outdoor fire. Place equal parts of pink salt, licorice root, and orris root in the dish.

Next, take your feather and identify the top portion that resembles an eye. Cut that portion out and discard the rest or store for future use. The spirit residue from a peacock can be used in glamours for seeking attention, attraction, and for increasing psychic abilities.

Place the eye on your forehead and hold it there with your index and middle fingers. Close your eyes and meditate. Imagine that you take on aspects of the peacock, having an array of beautiful feathers of your own. Imagine experiencing the feeling of grace and allure. Attract all the energy into you through your mind's eye.

Chant:

"I take on the poise of the peacock
I praise the spirits for this gift
To me, all eyes will flock
All attention will shift"

If you want attention from a specific person, work this into your chant and visualization. After the chant, repeat a mantra to help manifest the spell, like "Come to me." Be sure to always keep mantras short and memorable.

As you finish with your meditation, continue the mantra and gently place the eye on top of the other ingredients in the dish. Take a small amount of rum and pour it into the dish on top of the feather. Lastly, strike a match and toss it into the dish. As the ingredients burn, continue the mantra and do so until there is nothing left but ash. Recycle your ash at your crossroads during the next dark moon.

Exercise 5 – Expanding on Mirror Magick

We have used mirror magick in nearly all of our sections on glamour, whether it be for affirmations, masking, or for taking on deities like Aphrodite and the Morrigan. Though, there are also times when we need an instant brew version of magick. Good examples are given in *The Magic Mirror*.

"...Magic Mirror need not by any means be a mirror. People are also reported to have seen future and distant things in shining metal surfaces, in rock-crystals, and in glasses filled with water. The Old Testament mentions a divination made by the radiance of gems- where it speaks of Urim and Thummum, the breast-ornament of six bright and six dark stones which the high priest donned to receive revelations from Jehovah... Likewise in the Bible we find an instance of divination by means of polished metal cups; for according to the Septuagint, the cup that Joseph caused to be placed in the sack of Benjamin, was the cup from which he was wont to divine. Instead of cups, use was also made of metal balls, arrows, swords, knives, and metal mirrors." (Dessoir, 1890)

We can deduce from this passage that any reflective surface can be used in magick. The following experiment can be done anywhere. The below object is just an example, but the point of the exercise is to use any non-traditional mirrored surface in your mirror magick.

Magic mirror tropes have been around for centuries in mythology, poetry, and fiction. You may recall in Disney's *Snow White* that the evil queen uses a mirror for glamour magick to re-affirm her beauty. But the glamour fades when her own doubt shows the image of Snow White instead of her own.

Before we begin, start by noting your past experiences with mirror magick. If there are none, write down your preferred tool for divination and how you use it.

In this example, use an un-opened can of soda. I dare you to do this in a public place, like work. Let's say you're at your desk working away. But you find yourself getting easily distracted and are not having a productive day. You start to get overwhelmed.

Productivity Glamour

Take a can of soda and gaze into the reflective top. You will be doing a masking glamour. Take a minute or two to meditate on your reflection, then say the following chant in your head. Mental spells are just as powerful as those spoken aloud.

Chant:

"I am efficient and my work ethic high.
I won't bring work home tonight.
When my trance breaks, I will work hard.
I will stay on task and on guard."

At the end of your workday, take notes. Were you productive? If you didn't stay on task, why?

Kitchen Witch Glamour

In our section *Attract Energy, Not People*, we discussed glamour via the arts. I want to dedicate this section to different recipes you can use for your glamours. Even if you don't consider yourself a kitchen witch, these recipes are still fun to try!

Cooking is like any other art that is associated with glamour. Whether you have bad food or good food, meals are meant to be experienced. Food is a source that brings us energy and life. The smell of garlic roasting in a pan, warm bread rising in the oven, the sizzle of a burger on the grill—all this plays on our senses. It starts in our olfactory receptors while those delicious aromas are wafting in the air, then creates a whole new experience once you taste your food.

And like any other energy in glamour, we can manipulate this to suit our needs. The magick is in how we harvest our foods, how we prepare them, how we cook them, what ingredients we pair with them, and lastly, how we serve them. When working as a kitchen witch, *everything* is magick. We dedicate special knives and utensils to our cooking, cultivate special recipes and, if lucky, grow and process our own fresh ingredients.

Food is one of the most common offerings when working with deities and spirits in any culture. We give fae folk milk and honey. We provide our ancestors soul cakes. We break open a pomegranate for chthonic deities. Bread for Brigid. Wine for Dionysus. The list goes on.

But libation to the gods isn't the only way to incorporate magick into food. You can manipulate energy when cooking a family meal, at a dinner party, potluck, or meal for a special someone. A candlelit dinner soon becomes a ritual. Your evening glass of wine transforms into a shared libation to the hearth. When you start recognizing the magick of food, it's hard not to see it in every meal you make.

The following recipe is a basic one for crescent-shaped moon cakes in honor of the goddess Diana. I take reference from Charles Leland's *Aradia: Gospel of Witches*. (1899) In Leland's book, Diana is portrayed as a goddess to the poor and less fortunate. It is controversial, as her daughter Aradia is also the daughter of Lucifer.

Along with aiding the poor, Diana was also a goddess of love, sex, and lust. Aradia was tasked to go to Earth on a mission from her mother Diana, and with the success of that mission, promised the ability to grant love to her worshippers. Make these cakes for someone unobtainable you have an eye for.

Crescent Moon Cakes

Ingredients:
1 tsp honey
1/3 cup shortening, oil, or butter
½ cup brown sugar

1tbsp white wine
1 ½ cups flour
1/4 tsp baking soda
¼ tsp salt
1 ¼ cups oatmeal
Pinch of cloves, ginger, cinnamon, and allspice to taste

Instruction:
Preheat the oven to 350 degrees. Mix together the honey, shortening, brown sugar, and white wine in a bowl. Continue to stir and slowly add in the flour, baking soda, salt, and oatmeal. Add water as needed to form the dough.

Cut or roll the dough into crescent shapes and spread evenly along your baking sheet. Bake until golden or about fifteen minutes. Light a candle for Diana and chant the passage from Leland's work from the following page.

"You shall make cakes of meal, wine, salt and honey in the shape of a (crescent or horned) moon, and then put them to bake and say:

I do not bake the bread, nor with the salt
Nor do I cook the honey with the wine;
I bake the body and the blood and soul
The soul of Great Diana, that she shall
Know neither rest nor peace, and ever be
In cruel suffering till she will grant
What I request, what I do most desire,
I beg it of her from my very heart!
And if the grace be granted, Oh Diana!
In honor of thee I will hold this feast,

Feast and drain the goblet deep,
We will dance and wildly leap,
And if thou grant'st the grace which I require,
Then when the dance is wildest, all the lamps
Shall be extinguished and we'll freely love!"

(Leland, Original: 1899; Translation: 2010)

Dates have been a magickal food for centuries and are often associated with Mesopotamian mythology as offerings to Inanna. They are a healthy and nutritious source of quick energy with no downsides. Next time you are tempted to buy an energy drink or coffee, try snacking on a date instead. Many cultures that practice intermittent fasting include dates in their diet. These delicious morsels will have you full of energy, feeling great about yourself, and curb your appetite.

These fruits definitely have a unique taste and are something to get used to if not currently in your diet. Wrap them in bacon, mash them with nut butter into energy balls, or eat them plain. I prefer the following recipe, which to me tastes worthy of libation to Inanna.

Stuffed Medjool Dates

Ingredients:
Medjool dates
Pistachios
Goat cheese
Salt

Pepper
Smoked paprika
Honey

Instruction:

The best part about this snack is that there's no cooking required! Measurements are subjective depending on how many you are preparing. Start by taking your kitchen knife and partially slicing the dates to remove the pits. Set them aside. Next, remove the shells from your pistachios and crush them with a mallet or rolling pin.

Gently spoon the goat cheese into your dates. Make sure it is room temperature, so it is easier to work with. Sprinkle on salt and pepper along with a small touch of the smoked paprika. On top, pinch some of the crushed pistachios and add a drizzle of honey over the dates. Keep leftovers refrigerated if there are any!

If you are going for a masculine glamour, try working with Dionysus and cooking with grapes. Yes, they have uses other than wine. Still, wine is a great counterpart to any kitchen concoctions, whether they are magickal or not.

Did you know Romans used to dilute their wine with at least two parts water so they weren't tempted toward drunken and lustful shenanigans? It also helped stretch out the supply, considering wine was a common addition to breakfast, lunch, and dinner. What a concept.

What would your friends say if they saw you watering down your wine at brunch? And why don't people have wine at brunch anymore?

Roasted Grape Crostini

Ingredients:
Red grapes
Goat cheese
Honey
Baguette
Olive oil
Salt
Pepper
Thyme
Pecans
Balsamic vinegar

Instruction:

Okay, so Greeks and Romans didn't make crostini out of baguettes; they had freshly made loaves. But I promise you won't be disappointed.

Preheat your oven to 325 degrees. Rub a baking sheet with a generous amount of olive oil, mixing your grapes in the oil. Toss your seasoning on the grapes. (Salt, pepper, and thyme) Roast the grapes until caramelized. They should be done in about 45-50 minutes.

While cooking, prepare your baguette into even slices. Mash your pecans into crumbles that can be sprinkled over your crostini. In a small frying pan on medium heat, toast your bread slices in light olive oil. Use the leftover oil to toast your pecans. These cook and can burn quickly, which is why I recommend cooking them separately.

Use room temperature goat cheese and spread on the bread slices. Add your roasted grapes and pecans. Top with light drizzles of honey and balsamic vinegar before serving. I recommend pairing it with a red wine and to toast to Dionysus when you ask for his bounty and glamour. I wouldn't dilute his portion.

If you are affected by SAD (Seasonal Affective Disorder), try working with Saturn. Back when Saturnalia was celebrated commonly, there was an entire month of festivities in December. A mock king was named called the Lord of Misrule, usually from among peasants, to be treated as royalty with upscale feasts, women, and indulgence. At the end of Saturnalia, he was sacrificed to Saturn.

As witchcraft evolved, we now know that sacrifice doesn't equate to death. We make petitions, burn incense, use crystals, teas, blood, and bones, but the exchange of a life force isn't necessary for any spell. Try this winter root salad instead and share your feast with Saturn to be king for a day.

Salads usually give the feeling of spring with fresh iceberg lettuce, arugula, and romaine. Root vegetables are heartier, filling, and a must- have comfort food on a cold day. It will turn your SAD face upside right.

Winter Root Salad

Ingredients:
½ lb. purple carrots
½ lb. golden beets
½ tsp orange zest
2 tbsp orange juice
2 tbsp olive oil
½ tsp honey
½ tsp salt
¼ tsp pepper
¼ cup goat cheese
¼ cup pistachio
¼ cup fresh mint
2 tbsp champagne vinegar

Instruction:

Using a potato peeler, or if you're lucky, a Kitchenaid spiralizer, slice your beets and carrots into ribbons and toss them in a bowl. These are the roots of the salad. Toss and mix in goat cheese, mint leaves, and pistachios.

In a separate bowl, prepare your dressing. Whisk together the orange zest, orange juice, vinegar, honey, oil, salt, and pepper. You can keep this as a side dressing or mix into your salad directly. And above all, enjoy!

To get in touch with dark femininity or the dead, I always work with pomegranates in ritual. It was the fruit that trapped Persephone with Hades in the Underworld. It was the pomegranate, not the apple, that Eve feasted upon. Inanna stole the secret knowledge from The Huluppu Tree and infinite knowledge through the pomegranate. It's a sacred fruit and a must when working rituals on Samhain and anytime I invoke one of those goddesses.

So, I want to include a glamour recipe that will cloak you in the fierce fire of these dark goddess aspects. This glamour is for knowledge and sexual prowess. To walk the walk and talk the talk.

Huluppu Glazed Lamb Chops:

Ingredients:
1 rack of lamb chops
1 tbsp salt
1 tbsp pepper
1 tbsp rosemary
4 cloves garlic

3 ¾ cups pomegranate juice
¼ cup balsamic vinegar
¼ cup white sugar
¼ cup dark brown sugar
2 tbsp lemon juice
1 cup fresh pomegranate seeds
½ cup fresh mint leaves, finely chopped
2 tbsp pine nuts
A healthy amount of olive oil

Instruction:

First, we start by making the pomegranate glaze. On medium-high heat, add the pomegranate juice, balsamic vinegar, white sugar, lemon juice, and the brown sugar. Whisk together until it thickens into a syrup, then remove from heat to cool.

Next, set your grill on medium-high heat. Prepare the lamb by rubbing all sides with salt, pepper, and rosemary.

In a saucepan, bring olive oil to medium-high heat and roast your garlic cloves and pine nuts. While these are roasting, brush the glaze generously on the lamb chops.

Reduce the heat on the garlic and pine nuts. Grill your lamb for about three minutes per side depending on the thickness for rare to medium-rare, flipping only once and brushing on more of the pomegranate glaze. They should come out with a nice char. Garnish your lamb with pomegranate seeds, fresh mint, garlic, and pine nuts. Pair with your favorite red wine and enjoy!

A staple in nearly every kitchen is olive oil. Olives and olive oil specifically were sacred to ancient Greeks. The significance of olive oil comes from a story between Athena and Poseidon fighting over Athens. Athena planted the olive tree as a symbol of victory and dominance. In witchcraft today, olives represent prosperity, peace, rebirth, and determination. Even when the entire Acropolis city had been burned, the olive tree persisted and grew. Extending the olive branch is a symbol of peace in multiple cultures, even in the bible when a dove returns to Noah's ark holding an olive branch, as a messenger of peace.

For glamours in which you want to make amends or win a dispute, use olives. Here is a classic Mediterranean desert you can try to make, the olive oil cake. Cakes and ales are traditional offerings to most deities. This also makes for a good coffee cake or light dessert on any occasion.

Olive Oil Cake

Ingredients:
¼ tsp salt
¼ tsp baking soda
½ tsp baking powder
1 ¼ cups cake flour (sub; all-purpose)
2/3 cup white sugar
2/3 cup olive oil
½ cup Greek yogurt

¼ cup lemon zest
3 tbsp lemon juice
2 eggs

Instruction:
Grease a loaf pan or a 9" cake pan and preheat your oven to 350 degrees. In a large bowl, combine the salt, baking soda, baking powder, sugar, and flour. Slowly fold in the wet ingredients, including the yogurt, olive oil, zest, eggs, and lemon juice. Pour the cake batter into the pan and bake for 35 minutes or until done. As the cake bakes, infuse your glamour with the following chant.

Chant:

"As this treat sets to bake
May peace be infused within this cake
Like the olives from Athena's tree
I'll reap rewards that come to me"

In ancient Egypt, food offerings were given each day to please the gods. The pharaohs would make a selection of the finest fowl, fruits, and vegetables and have peasants bless the ingredients with water, incense, and natron. Food would be left daily at a shrine in exchange for the prosperity and health of their community. These offerings would later be shared among priests, while bread and grain were left at the altar.

Instead of natron, we will use salt in our recipes. Salt has a long history of purification and magical purposes. Like salt, natron was also a natural preservative that was used in foods and mummification. It cleanses the body and was utilized in cleansing homes. In modern-day cooking, we still tend to have a heavy hand with salt when seasoning our food.

Other popular ingredients of ancient Egypt include garlic, leeks, green onion, cabbage, turnips, and legumes. Fowl like duck, pigeon, and goose were considered rich poultry. For more common folk, they prepared crane, swan, and ostrich. Eggs were also an important protein.

For a prosperity glamour, try working with Hapi. Hapi was worshipped for bringing on the annual flood of the Nile each year and was responsible for the fertile natron salt deposits.

Below is a duck recipe as a libation to Hapi for prosperity. Remember, prosperity is more than wealth. It is success, luck, and abundance. When working this glamour, keep in mind the big picture, not actual money. In ancient Egypt, prosperity was having the water to allow your crops to grow and to yield large harvests to support your family.

Hapi Duck

Ingredients:
2 whole ducks, skin scored
1 tbsp salt
3 large leeks
7 tbsp butter
5 garlic cloves
1 cup cream
¼ cup chicken stock
1 cup grated parmesan

Instruction:
Preheat your oven to 350 degrees for your duck.
Prepare the fowl by rubbing the salt between the scores
in the skin. While rubbing in the salt, work your magick.
Say the following chant to Hapi.

Chant:
"As above and so below
Bless this fowl with salt
Like the Nile, overflow
As the lore of the occult

Allow those who feast with me today
To prosper in every way
Hapi, let us bask in happiness
May all who consume my meal be in bliss"

Further Instruction:
Roast the duck for about 1 ½ hours. While resting,
prepare the leeks. Chop them and fry them in butter
over stovetop until soft, between 5-10 minutes. Then,
add your garlic, cream, and stock to the pan. Simmer for
15 minutes. Remove the leeks from the heat and add in
the parmesan. Spoon the creamy leeks over the duck to
serve.

Exercise 6 – The Power of Poppets

As an alternative to mirror magick, poppets are a great way to manifest glamour. This is a nice option for those with aphantasia or who have a hard time with visualization. With a poppet or any other symbolic object that's consecrated to your purpose, you have a nice visual representation to put your focus on.

A poppet can be constructed from almost anything. It's a visual representation of a person and resembles a small doll. Traditionally, they are made from corn husks, twigs and twine, or yawn. Create a poppet for a person you want to glamour. This is more than likely yourself. Because of the amount of work that goes into making one, it's best to use the poppet more than once. Though you can always un-bind a person from a poppet if you wish to use it for other purposes.

Found in many Egyptian tombs between the sixth and thirteenth dynasties were what we now call paddle dolls. They are believed to have been used to invoke Hathor, a goddess of fertility and affection. Their hair was made of beads and the paddle decorated with paints.

(G. Pinch, Votive offerings to Hathor [Oxford 1993], p.217;
N. Strudwick, Masterpieces of Ancient Egypt, London 2006, pp. 74-5. Strudwick N 2006–Image credited to the British Museum of London)
(Unknown, Masterpieces of Ancient Egypt)

Although paddle dolls aren't traditionally called poppets, the term poppet was meant to describe a doll or smile child. The Greeks used something similar called kolossoi. In *Pharmakeutria,* (Approx. 200BDE) Theocritus uses glamour with kolossoi by making them of wax and melting them to seal the spell.

(Image of various kolossoi, sourced from https://libguides.brooklyn.cuny.edu/magicancient world/greece_gallery)

(Unknown, From Left to Right: Angels & Demons: Jewish Magic Through the Ages, Keramikos & Bronze Kolossos, Hellenistic, Bronze)

For our glamour, we will take a more modern approach to poppets. The following is what you will need for your base. The stuffing is entirely up to you, but I will give an example.

Before we begin, reflect on your favorite doll or toy you had as a kid. Why was it special? Write about a memory of this toy.

NOTES

_____
_____
_____
_____
_____
_____
_____
_____
_____
_____
_____
_____

Supplies:
1 piece of card stock
2 pieces of felt
Scissors
Cotton balls or beads
Marker
Choice of needle/thread, hole puncher/yarn or a stapler (I don't judge)

Just keep in mind the contents of your poppet when deciding how to construct the base. You don't want the contents to fall out, and you don't want them to rot.

Start out by drawing a simple human-shaped figure on your piece of card stock. It should be the shape of a gingerbread man, nothing too extravegent. Next, cut out the outline. Take two pieces of felt and line them up. Use color coordination when selecting your material in order to enhance your spell.

Next, place your person cutout on top of the two pieces of felt. You will use the card stock as a guide to cut out two symmetrical pieces of felt. Once you have two cutouts of the same shape and size, it's time to sew your poppet shut. Use needle and thread, a hole puncher and yarn, or even a stapler. As long as it stays shut, the medium doesn't matter. Leave a small hole open so you can stuff your poppet with contents to represent your spell.

Put in herbs, trinkets, notes, and fill the rest with cotton balls or beads as filler.

In this example, we will dedicate a poppet to ourselves. Some people have entire self-care altars. But all you need is one thing that represents you. Use your marker to draw a face and inscribe any types of sacred symbols you wish. It could be a heart, a pentacle, runes, etc.

You can even give yourself hair with yarn or twine. Maybe you want to use beads like the ancient egyptians did. You can even include some pieces of your own hair. Do something that represents your personal creativity.

When you're done glamourizing your poppet, it's time to select the stuffing. Here is an example of what I would stuff into my poppet and why.

Ingredients:
Dried rose petals
Dried jasmine flowers
Clear beads
Small amethyst point
A note on positive affirmations

I chose rose petals and jasmine, first of all, because they are my favorite flowers to use in my craft. Secondly, roses are symbolic of love. If you make a poppet of yourself, it's important to base it on some level of self-care. Jasmine represents love as well but also promotes purity, sensuality, and wisdom.

Clear beads are just used as filler. You can realistically use packing peanuts and it wouldn't matter. It depends on the weight and feeling you want from your poppet when you hold it.

Amethyst is my favorite crystal because it represents so many things. I added it to my poppet for heightened awareness on my spiritual journey and to stimulate prophetic dreams. And the last ingredient is the most important. It's a special note for yourself to boost you up when you need it.

As you know, the affirmations we tell ourselves aren't traits we necessarily believe about ourselves. It's what we want to *manifest*. So next time you're down, hold onto your poppet and you will manifest the glamour of the traits you wrote down.

Once you have all of your ingredients in the poppet, seal it all the way up. This is subjective, but you could dab a bit of your favorite essential oil on the surface. And lastly, dedicate the poppet to yourself through a spell and give them a home on your altar or their own space.

The following is a spell I would give mine.

Chant:

"I bless this poppet to share my spirit
To boost me with truths I won't admit

I bind the sacred words within it
To endorse kinder habits

I vow to treat myself as I do this doll
And be open to my spirit's call"

To activate the poppet, you must give it a name. It is as simple as adding a line to your chant like, "I name you _____." After you speak its name into existence, you need to activate the poppet. To do this, breathe into it through where its mouth would be, or kiss it. Through this, you are transmuting your energy to awaken to doll.

Take my example and write your own spell of binding. It's important that what you write is unique to you. Write down some of your favorite herbs, crystals, and things about yourself below. Brainstorm some ideas for your personal poppet.

Another great medium for a poppet is clay. Sure, you can grab some cans of Play-Doh from the store, but there's something special about kneading the clay yourself. It works the same as kneading dough for kitchen witches. When it's created with your hands, when it's raw, the spell is much more potent.

Clay Poppet Recipe

There are many different recipes for making clay. I will offer a simple base. Once it's made and the texture you want, then you can fold in objects that represent your poppet. You can fold in personal effects of the person it's meant to manifest, like fingernails, blood, or hair. You can also include scents and associated essential oils. Do what feels right. Just be sure to add it to the mixture after the clay has been made.

Clay Recipe:

1 cup cornstarch
2 cups baking soda
1 ¼ cups water

This recipe can be air dried, or you can monitor it in the oven at a low temperature for several hours. I like to put mine outside in the elements, particularly under a dark moon.

When putting life into a clay poppet, it starts at the molding. If you want to influence someone's thoughts, put a small note and roll it into the head of the poppet. If you want this person to stop sucking your energy, for example, rub citronella oil on it like you are warding off a giant mosquito.

Poppets of yourself are also best made with clay. Mold yourself into someone you want to be. Put your heart into it. Figuratively, of course.

If you are working on a binding between you and someone else, I'd also suggest clay poppets. Use strands of their hair and yours and bind the clay hands together. If you can't obtain their hair, get creative. Use a string and manifest their energy into it.

When working with liminal magick, we respect and honor both light and dark, life and death. That's why the death card represents birth. It's a cycle. When breathing life into a clay poppet, I like to give it a burial to return it to the earth to be born. A small wooden box is ideal, but a shoebox works too.

Place it in the box and have a small burial for the poppet. I leave the death card from my tarot deck in the box as well. Do this under the dark moon. As you do so, bury the box with your intent in mind and imagine trapping the spirit. Mark the soil with a rock so you can find your place the next morning. When the poppet has served its purpose, you can return it to the earth and not look back after its final burial. I like to include a coin as a sacrifice to the spirit energy that possessed the poppet.

The coin is symbolic of the toll needed to enter the underworld in Greek mythology. In history, coins were placed in the deceased's mouth as an offering to Charon to guide them through River Styx in the underworld. The coin also acts as a seal and prevents the spirit from returning to the world of the living.

Exercise 7 – Sex Magick

Sex is definitely an act you want to feel glamourous in. People are often afraid of this topic, talking about it only behind closed doors or not at all in the home. In most magick practices and Pagan beliefs, sex is ritualized and sacred. We don't shame people for being sensual and having sexual prowess. Rather, it's encouraged.

While having your own glamour on you during sex is fine on its own, let's talk about putting a glamour on the environment first. Get out your entire arsenal of witchy tools, including candles, crystals, teas, oils, and incense. In sex magick, we want to overwhelm the senses to take us to a higher state of being. You're not just swapping fluid; you're feeding on each other's energies.

Sex magick has long been practiced but hasn't been a topic of discussion until the last century or so. Take Tantra, for example, and Indian practice that dates back to 300-400CE.

The word literally means 'woven together.' On the next page is a picture of the Tantric deity, Bhairava, a dark aspect of Shiva. He is also known as the masculine form of the great and powerful dark goddess, Kali. In his mythos, he severed the head of Brahma and was cursed to keep his skull as a begging bowl.

A little background: Both Brahma and Shiva were a part of the Hindu sacred trinity along with Vishnu. Bhairava was worshipped for many things but known for being a guardian to women in need of protection. He is also worshipped to achieve a state of hyper-awareness. When worshipping these deities, we recognize the sacred union of the divine masculine and feminine. We embrace our desires and actualize our highest potential. We look inward to transcend beyond the means of the physical world and embrace fulfillment.

If you want to include Bhairava and Kali in your rituals, meditate in a ritual bath beforehand. Suggested offerings include:

Cashews
Honey
Roses
Coconut
8-Pointed Star (To represent his eight aspects)

(Nadu)

Sex is more than just physical intimacy when we
talk about using it in a ritualistic sense. The act of
incorporating magick into sex is like a contract to
bind yourself to someone, or to bind them to you.
Your most primal urges are embraced, and you

take on godform of deities that represent divine masculine and divine feminine.

I want to clarify that this is far beyond traditional male and female relationships. We all have femininity and masculinity within us, and during these rituals, we often have a balance between the two with our partner. These energies are always spinning within us, just sometimes one more than the other. That's why so many of our deities we worship have male/female counterparts. Like the gods, we evolve. We change. We transcend. Your body is a temple. It's okay to worship yourself.

When partaking in godform during this type of rite, I often take on the aspect of Cernunnos when embracing the divine masculine. When I want to evoke the divine feminine within me, I like to take on the aspect of Hekate. Both deities thrive on indulgence and self-awareness.

During this godform, it is common to see the cycle of katabasis through the deity. Most myths have a story of a god sacrificing his life or it ending abruptly, and his partner goddess descending to the underworld or into another state of being. These patterns between mythos teach us wisdom, sacrifice, and to appreciate companionship. Choose deities that resonate with you to embody, not necessarily the divine pairings from the traditional stories. For example, you may work closely with Inanna, but you may have never worked with Tammuz before.

When you take on these deities, they teach you to be humble. They teach you not to have shame for indulgence. They teach you it's okay to love and be intimate, and that those two concepts don't always need to interlock.

Before giving ritual ideas, journal your thoughts on intimacy and how you would use it in your craft.

NOTES

Share your intent of this sacred rite with your partner. Get their consent to share energies and to partake in this bond with you. The point isn't to entrap someone in a relationship with you, it's to create a bond of trust, intimacy, and spirituality. Someone giving their energy to you willingly is much different from extracting it from someone.

Discuss the deities you want to take on in the rite. Discuss how you will represent the divine union. In my experience, me and my partner would both choose a deity. Then we would invoke them. We would re-live their mythos of katabasis representing the god's sacrifice and the goddess's journey to the underworld.

This isn't required, but I personally incorporate essence magick into my rite. Essence magick is when the sacrifice comes from yourself, whether it's in the form of blood, sweat, saliva, ejaculatory fluids, etc. This increases the potency of the spell and strengthens the bond even more. Not a lot is needed for this effect.

Before partaking in the exchange of essence with anyone, make sure to take safety precautions. Don't be reckless in the heat of the moment and not ask the right questions. Your health is the number-one priority above all else. To extract blood essence, I have a dedicated blade/athame. I suggest you use the same if you partake in essence magick. Here is a dedication rite.

Bonded Blade Dedication

Chant:

"I imbue this blade with my essence.
I use blood to bind my sacred bond,
To be in perfect trust in my partner's presence
I use this dagger as my wand."

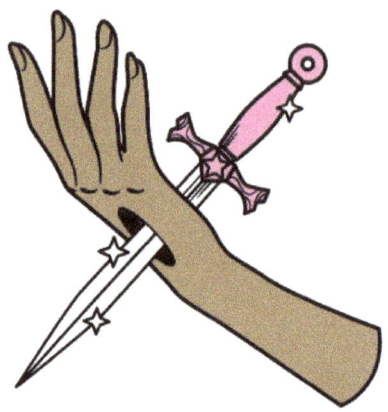

Sex Magick Exercise with Partner

Anoint the blade with blood or any other essence of your choosing. Just edit the chant if you use something else. Now you choose the sacred place. It could be a place you have already dedicated. A common choice is outdoors. Be sure if you choose this option that you have complete privacy. You don't want hikers in the woods to stumble upon you.
You definitely don't want an indecent exposure charge.

Supplies:
Candles (Red and black)
Incense

Crystals
Dedicated blade

You'll notice that I didn't give specifics on the types of incense and crystals to use or the quantities of candles. This is all personalized. The only thing that's a must is balance. Use an even number of candles. Light two incenses: one that represents you and one that represents your partner. Use a variety of crystals that associate with your root chakra, heart chakra, third eye, balance, and sensuality. Just ensure that you and your partner have an equal amount.

Instruction:

Place the candles around your sacred space. Practice fire safety when doing so. If you have enough candles and space, have them surround you and your partner in a circle. Add crystals if you wish. You and your partner take turns lighting the candles. Disrobe. Take hold of your chosen incense and a match and have your partner grab theirs. Light their incense.

Chant:

"I evoke your energy
Your angels and your demons
I evoke your everything
Both now and then"

Your partner is to say the same chant and light your incense as well. Set the incense aside and let the two aromas waft together. Mediate for a moment in each other's presence. Now, evoke the element of fire. Both can recite this verse.

Chant:

"I evoke the element of Fire
Twin flames cusped in desire
Like smoke, our spirits lifted higher
Our lights never brighter"

Now it's time to take godform. To invoke your chosen deities and re-enact their sacrifices in sacred intimacy.

The following is an example invocation to Inanna, also giving ode to other similar goddesses. Following that one is an invocation to Pan, a horned god. These invocations can also be found in my *Book of Invocations*.

Chant:

"Inanna

Daughter of love and skies
Sweet songs & lullabies
Prowling lioness
Loyal goddess

Names of many
Ishtar, Astarte, Aphrodite
All in one, I call unto thee

I honor your bravery
Desire & intensity

Time altered journey
Of strain and fertility

Your Underworld travels
We honor each season
As days unravel
You are our reason

I invoke thee Inanna
Into my compass
Isis, Diana
Become among us"

"Pan

Gallant, grove stomping
Glorious Pan
Hooves of goat,
Face of man

Through caves untold
Thy mysteries shown
Thy actions bold
As man does groan

You are the sun
And the ground beneath my feet
You are the one
Of verdant vine, rich and sweet

Wise and wond'rous
Holy beast
Pious, righteous
God of feasts

By furtive hand
You take the land

By summer end
Thy will does bend

With ceding grace
Thou plant thy seed
So we may face
The spring thou heed

By the light of the faithful flame
I call unto thee by name

By the symbol of sacred birch
My third eye open in eager search

O' mighty, beastly, loving Pan
Take my hand and join back your land

I invite thee to my runic round
I invoke thee by music – spellbound"

After each of you has invoked your respective
deities, this is the time to optionally share essence.
Carefully and gently use your dedicated blade.
Allow your partner to consume your essence and
then, in turn, do the same to theirs.

Briefly meditate on how you feel as your deity. Let
your primal take over. Engage in intimacy. Do so at
least until your chosen candles have burned out. If
possible, sleep under the stars together once done.
The next day, note your experiences.

NOTES

After this exercise, you should feel a sense of oneness. Oneness with your partner and with the divine. There is such a stigma on open communication about sensuality. Let's change that.

If you don't have a partner or want one, you can still participate in sex magick. You have a goddess in you begging to come out. Take time to get to know yourself. You can still use godform by yourself. A solo option would be to manifest a deity that possesses an energy you are lacking at that moment. One that compliments you.

For example, I primarily harness feminine energy. Though, sometimes I like to feel grounded and bathe in that masculine energy I crave. This is when I would invoke Cernunnos to get in touch with that beastly energy. You can use the same chants and spellwork as you would have with a partner. But this time, get in touch with the divine and your higher sense of self.

There are definitely more simple ways to incorporate sex magick in your glamour. Like sigil work, you burn a desire in your mind and seal it. In this case, sealing is the point of orgasm. Sex magick can be performed for anything you want to come to fruition, but it's best used in relation to physical and social desires.

The reason sex magick is successful and that it's so potent when paired with glamour magick is because it works through pheromones. Think of pheromones as your natural perfume. It's a chemical that makes hormones go wild and can influence yourself or your partner through intimate suggestion.

While having the power of pheromones at play, essence magick through ejaculation and your glamour active, that is a sure recipe for success. Like burning a note with your intentions or burying your spell, alternatively, you can release that energy through sex if you have an open mind. Here's an example. No supplies. No need to chant, even. Just doing.

Climax Magick

Instruction:
This ritual can be done with yourself through masturbation or with a partner. Before you initiate intimacy, keep in mind your intentions of making this a ritual versus your general sexual endeavors. Come up with a singular word or short phrase you can turn into a mantra. This can be chanted during sex, or more often, exclaimed loudly in your mind.

Your partner doesn't need to be aware of this type of spell, nor do they need to help. But if they want to, all the better. Just because you treat intimacy spiritually doesn't mean your sexual partners should ever feel forced or obliged to partake in ritual. Having a repetitive phrase you can say in your head works just fine and doesn't have to affect your partner in any way. When riding solo, this isn't something you need to worry about.

If you prefer visualization, you can let your mind wander to create your own sigil or symbol that represents your intent. Try not to make it too complex. In your heightened state of awareness, you won't be able to have complex chains of visual thoughts.

You still want to be mindful of your partner if you have one and keep your focus on them and their pleasure as well. If you are struggling to keep focus and balance on both your partner and your mantra, let the mantra go and table the ritual for another day. If you don't get to the end and release, the spell won't work.

At the height of the rising action, let go of your mantra and get lost in intimacy. Indulge in the essence of the magick. Feel the power in your veins and spirit until your mind melts. This seals the spell. If you follow the path of chaos, you would at this point forget the mantra completely and put it into your unconscious. I don't agree with this, as in my belief, in order to manifest, you need to work all levels of consciousness into witchcraft. Though, I would encourage you to do what speaks to you.

Exercise 8 – Subconscious Commands with Sigils

In Creating a Safe Space, we learned a little bit about sigils and how we use them to change the glamour of our environment. We're now going to delve deeper into the manipulation aspects of glamour and how to use sigils to influence other people.

The creation of our sigils will be in the same format for the purpose of consistency in this exercise. If that way doesn't speak to you, feel free to freeform and draw whatever comes to mind when meditating on your command. With our painted rocks, we applied a permanent sigil. We are going to try sealing through the act of destroying the symbol. We will manifest by means of sealing the symbol into our subconscious mind.

Like we do with all our exercises, let's start by journaling our thoughts. List some simple commands based on minor changes you want in your life. Remember, this exercise is to influence others through glamour, so you can't target concepts like winning the lottery.

Commands with Sigils

When working on commands, start out with simple phrases first. Work up to more specifics the more you get comfortable manifesting through sigils. I'll get personal with this suggestion, and we'll use getting this book being successful as my command. While it would be a good chuckle to spell a publisher into loving my manuscript, I don't think they would appreciate the sentiment.

Make your command unique to a mundane situation you possess. Glamour your boss into bringing in doughnuts on Monday. Glamour your professor into grading your written report well. Glamour the cute guy at the coffee shop into noticing you today and striking up conversation. Keep it simple.

Here is my example phrase of power:

MY BOOK WILL BE SUCCESSFUL

As we did previously, we'll strike out all the vowels and consonants that appear more than once. This isn't the formula for success, just a method that works. Be as creative as you want. The letters I have left look like this:

MY B~~OO~~K W~~ILL~~ ~~BE~~ ~~SUCCESSFUL~~

MYBKWLSCF

While meditating on your intention, draw your letters to form an abstract picture. And because we're destroying the symbol to seal it, it can be ugly! The more you practice, the cooler they will eventually look.

See the following picture for my sigil. Take as much artistic liberty as you want to transform your line art into an unrecognizable symbol. This method is only meant to be a guide to get your creative juices flowing.

MY BOOK WILL BE SUCCESSFUL

After you're happy with your sigil, transfer it to birch bark or an object that's safe to burn in a bowl or cauldron. I use birch to manifest my desires since it represents rebirth, new beginnings, realm travel, and opportunity. Usually, any desire I'm trying to manifest coordinates with one of those attributes of birch.

Take one last good look at your symbol and burn it into your subconscious, along with your phrase of power. Hold it over your bowl and prepare your match. Then light it and let it burn completely.

Either keep the contents in your dish until your desire manifests or throw it at the crossroads during the next new moon. The new moon is best for manifesting a strong change in your life.

Save this tactic for bigger glamours. Maybe not your boss bringing in doughnuts.

Another option to seal this spell is to take the ashes and put them on the path of the person you are glamouring. Drop them by their car, their house, or somewhere they like to go. Be sure to dispose of the remnants outside so the ashes return to the earth. I don't think anyone would appreciate birch ash on their desk at work or in their brand-new car. You also don't want to be in a position to explain yourself to that person.

Sigils are a fun way to manifest glamour. Some other ideas to seal your sigils are sidewalk chalk, cooking oil in kitchen witchery, essential oil on your skin, or even tracing them in air with a stick of sage. The possibilities are endless.

Now use the space below to draw your own sigil. Pick from the list you made above.

Insert your art here:

Another way to seal your sigil is by drawing it on your body. And while a tattoo may sound like a really cool idea, that's not what I mean. We are going to make things a lot simpler. You just need waterproof eyeliner. Using makeup just adds that glamour oomph, and it's safe for your skin.

You can put your sigil on your wrist, so you're always reminded of it. Or if you prefer to forget about it and lock it into your subconscious, you can put it anywhere. Grab a friend and have them draw it on your back. You do you! In the next exercise, we'll learn the history of makeup in magick and give you more example spells.

Exercise 9 – Makeup Spells

Sex symbols have long been represented through wearing red lipstick and having dark liner cat eyes. As we learned in the beginning of this book, red is the color of sex. And sex sells. It has been selling in pop culture for nearly one hundred years; look back to the cartoon Betty Boop that aired in the 1930's, for example. The Marilyn Monroe effect features Marilyn in her iconic red lips that she rocked in the 1950's.

But makeup has been around much longer than only the past few centuries. Look at the relics we have of ancient Egypt and their fearless leaders, such as Nefertiti and Cleopatra. Nefertiti's name literally means 'the beautiful one has come.' It was definitely a name to live up to.

They made bold statements with their makeup and used the resources of the Earth to create pigment. It was not only a symbol of power; it was glamour, ritual magick. The artistic designs would command attention and make servants be envious. It gave these leaders confidence and power. And their stories were carried through the arts into hieroglyphics, imprinting their spells in stone and clay to be preserved for thousands of years to come.

Do you wear makeup? Why or why not? How do you feel with it on?

In glamour magick, your makeup is your wand. We will start with a ritual to imbue power into your lipstick. The type of energy we want to evoke is sensual aggression. When you wear this lipstick, you won't take no for an answer. We will enchant your words to be alluring and persuasive. Your root chakra must be firmly planted to seal this spell.

Lips of a Siren

Supplies:

Red lipstick
Handheld mirror
Salt
Herbs associated with persuasion (Try cilantro,
licorice root, or orris root)
3 tealight candles

Instruction:

Place the mirror on a flat surface with the reflective
side pointed up. Stand up the lipstick in the center
of the mirror. Take your tealight candles and
arrange them in an equilateral triangle around the
lipstick, with the point facing away from you.

In a circle around the candles, sprinkle the salt and
herbs. Light the candles and hold out your palms
toward the flames. Imagine pouring your energy
into the circle. That energy with the flames and the
power of the herbs is being sent to the lipstick in
three neat ley lines from the candles. After you are
focused, speak the following chant.

Chant:

"From my roots through the palms of my hands
I'm the fruit sought out by many men

I enchant this makeup
To my lips
As the Queen of Cups
I shall eclipse

Any desire to tell me no
As above and so below

My every command is your wish
As long as red sits upon my lips"

Dispose of the herbs and clean up your space afterward. The lipstick can be stored anywhere. When you wear it, you will have the power of persuasion.

This next spell is to command presence in a room. We will use eyeliner as the conduit for this spell. I call this one 'All Eyes on Me.'

All Eyes on Me

Supplies:

Eyeliner (Liquid works best)
Herbs associated with attraction (Cloves, cinnamon sticks)
Passionflower (Holistic remedy for healthy eyesight and metaphysically used for beauty and deception)
Censer
Charcoal (For burning incense)
Resin (Dragon's blood, copal, frankincense)
Red candle

Instruction:

Take your eyeliner and your candle. You are going to draw either a sigil to represent attraction and attention, a visual image like an eye, or simply write 'ALL EYES ON ME.' Place the candle behind the censer so when the censer is lit, the smoke rises from behind the candle. Place the eyeliner in front of the candle.

Now, prepare your loose incense. Put the charcoal on the censer and add resin as the base. This keeps your incense smoking. Then, add the herbs and passionflower. (Note: If you are using cinnamon sticks, you can grind them prior to the ritual with a mortar and pestle.) Light the charcoal and meditate for a moment.

Focus on your root chakra and imagine a red light emanating from your spine, with branches and roots growing like a tree throughout your body.

Once you are grounded and feel the strength of your root chakra at full potential, light the red candle. Focus on your symbol or words at the base of the candle. Concentrate on results and manifestation. You should feel a complete sense of control.

We are going to call on the deity Bast or Bastet, whom you manifest as a cat.

Chant:

"May this liner paint my eyes so that
None can look away
With eyes of the cat, I call to Bast
To play predator and prey

When donned in black
I become the cat
I am the Eye of Ra

All eyes on me
I will be
The envy of them all"

Let the candle naturally extinguish as you burn the symbol or written phrase in your head. Like the lipstick, this eyeliner can be stored anywhere for later use. Whenever you need to get someone's attention, whether it be for romantic reasons or any reason at all, wear it proudly. Take on the power of Bast and the Eye of Ra.

After trying out these spells, pick a piece of makeup that's your favorite or one you think suits you best. It can be anything: eye shadow, concealer, blush, etc.

Try writing your own glamour spell using the chosen makeup.

Supplies:

_____

_____

_____

Instruction:

_____

_____

_____

_____

_____

_____

Chant:

_____

_____

_____

_____

_____

Exercise 10 – Banes and Bitchcraft

This is the eff around and find out exercise. Don't be afraid to be human. If you've learned anything from this book so far, I hope it's that. We all have banes we deal with, whether they manifest as people, thoughts, or things. Luckily, we don't have to put up with that shit.

'An ye harm none' is a law I abided by for a long time. Wiccans, I have a deep respect for your path. I was on it for many years. If hexing is against your morals, don't practice the exercises in this passage. But for the purpose of understanding and learning, I encourage you to read it, anyway.

You're still here? Good. For everything in your life that feels out of your control, that you actually can't control, that's a bane. A bane is anything that causes harm. This could be emotionally or physically. It can even be a thing that results in death. That is why we label poisonous herbs as baneful.

Most times, we can banish our banes. But maybe that isn't enough. To banish isn't the same as teaching a lesson. This is the part where we nudge karma in the right direction. You can cut the cord, but would you cut the leash off a rabid dog? I think not.

Write about some things that bother you that you can't control. A time a person has wronged you. A time when words made you feel physically ill.

NOTES

This is the part where I give you a spiel on ethics. Unfortunately, there are many gatekeepers in witchcraft, but you won't be guarded by any gates here. Everyone has their own personal code of ethics, and anyone who has considered casting a curse is aware of what's appropriate and justified. I can't give you a list of reasons that are okay to curse someone and list what's not okay. Everyone marches to the beat of their own drum. Individuality and circumstance determine what's necessary to keep that drum beating.

Curses don't always involve hot-footing and royally messing up someone's life. The best curses teach lessons and are subtle. We call it bitchcraft here in good humor, to keep the conversation light. We can't heal those who drain us. We simply must draw a line.

Glamour doesn't discriminate. We glamour the good, the bad, and the ugly. And trust me, things are about to get ugly. Here's a glamour to make someone who's ugly on the inside have the carpet to match the drapes.

Justice

Supplies:
Person-shaped candle (Can be found at any metaphysical store)
Ritual dagger or carving tool
Justice tarot card

Instruction:
This spell is simple. The candle here is the conduit to transfer the glamour onto the target. The candle is your poppet. At the bottom of the candle, take your carving tool and carve the name of the person. Take a moment to meditate on this person and all the nasty things they've done to you. Place the tarot card in front of the candle.

When you light the candle, the wax will start dripping down from the face. This will be symbolic of their beauty melting away to reveal their ugly inside. The chant below is to Nemesis, the Greek goddess of justice. You, however, can choose any deity or force that you want. You can even just address the concept of 'justice.'

<u>Chant</u>:

"Nemesis, I call ye hence
To charge _____ with great offense

As the wax melts away
Their beauty fades

And now their pretty face
Will cause them to be disowned

May _____ learn from their mistakes
Only then can beauty be restored
When they stop acting fake
This injustice can't be ignored"

When hexing, I intentionally always make my spells contingent upon learning a lesson. Because other than just making us feel good, plain old revenge doesn't solve a problem. So be sure when messing with bitchcraft, you don't lose your purpose. Purpose and intent need to be aligned.

Write about how you feel about 'black' magick and your experiences. Alternatively, write about a time you learned a lesson from a mistake.

Everyone in life has been taught a lesson. We've all had the chance to level up from our experiences. That doesn't stop us from occasionally putting on rose-colored glasses. Sometimes we cling onto the miniscule good things in people that don't deserve recognition. We idolize people that straight up tear us down.

I'm guessing you've had a friend that was dating someone who treated them completely awful. They knew it but still wanted to see the good in them? Yeah. I've been on both ends of the stick. While you may want to give your friend a good ol' slap in the back of the head, that's not going to teach them anything besides not to tell you shit anymore. Instead, let's try a glamour to show someone's true colors.

Unfortunately, there is no contingency here. Your friend is bound to be hurt. But this is ripping off a Band-Aid compared to a slow chisel at the heart. Sometimes truth hurts.

Simply Sour Seer Jar

Supplies:
Mason jar
½ cup apple cider vinegar
3 tablespoons cooking oil (Your choice)
Food coloring (Your choice of color)
Red chime candle

Instruction:
In a container, add the apple cider vinegar and in another have the oil. Put a drop or two of food coloring in the oil and mix. The oil represents the target's bad intentions. Vinegar is used for banishment, protection, and meddling love spells. It's the perfect conduit for highlighting someone's negative qualities to protect a friend in need. The red represents love and relationships, which is why we use this color for coordination rather than black, the common hexing color coordination.

Take the ingredients over to your sacred space. Add the vinegar to the jar first, then the colored oil.

Seal the jar with the lid. Next, grab the chime candle and hold the end over the middle of the mason jar lid. Take your match and let the hot wax drip onto the lid. Rotate the candle so that the bottom remains flat.

Quickly and firmly, place the candle onto the hot wax and hold it for twenty seconds. This should seal the candle in place upright. We are not using a holder, because when we light the candle, we want the wax to drip over the jar and to even further seal the jar. Once this is done, light the candle.

Chant:

"This is the time, here in this moment
For my friend to end this brutal torment

To see their partner makes them ill
That they have eyes set to kill

That drains them of their energy
That their partner's intentions are truly ugly

This oil represents their evils
May they see this and end things, quick and civil

Show _____ for who they really are
The charade they play won't get them far

Like the wax of this candle
May it melt and fizzle"

Let the candle burn out completely. Don't leave open flames unattended. The next time your friend is in despair over their partner, activate the spell by shaking the jar. By doing this, your glamour will soon manifest. Make sure your willpower is stronger than your friend's stubbornness.

We all have magick, and a lover scorned holds immense power. If this happens and you feel like your spell isn't working, don't worry. It will. Great things take time. Whenever a new situation arises, shake the jar again and re-focus your intentions.

Another good combination for a sour jar spell is to add garlic and lemon to the apple cider vinegar. These ingredients will yield the same result. Instead of adding the oil, peel a lemon and drop the fruit into the jar before sealing, then discard the scraps or use later in a simmer pot. Peeling the lemon represents taking the target's outer layers off and revealing their sour insides. Replace your chant with something like this. Instead of:

"This oil represents their evils
May they see this and end things, quick and civil"

Try:

"This lemon shows their sour soul
Where there should be a heart is a hole"

Another common hex is a *"shut them up"* spell. We all know someone who has a mouth that doesn't have a filter. These people are sharp with their tongues to make a joke at the expense of other people's feelings. The best way to handle these situations is to go to the root of the problem. We're going to help them shut up.

This glamour is the illusion that they can't speak. We cast a spell to make their mouths feel heavy and their lips swollen. Talking becomes taxing to the target, and their jokes don't give them those warm belly laughs anymore. We'll put a contingency on this one because I believe these people can change.

Shut Them Up

Supplies:
Felt poppet
Scissors
Needle
Thread

Instruction:
See the previous exercise on poppets for how to construct one of felt. Use your scissors to snip a hole to make an open mouth. Thread the needle and have it ready. While saying the below chant, you are going to sew its mouth shut. Before you do so, declare the name of the poppet as the target and breathe life into it by blowing in its mouth or giving it a kiss.

When you are done doing the chant, seal the spell by cutting the string, tying it, and then sticking the needle horizontally through its mouth. When you

feel that the target has learned their lesson,
remove the needle and cut the stitches open.

"I curse you _____ to seal your lips
Until you learn some empathy
I'll no longer let your tongue slip
I'll take away your apathy
And only with apology
Your stitches will be snipped
Your energy in this effigy
Your fate in my fingertips"

Keep the poppet somewhere safe and discrete.
Don't bury it and forget about it. I suggest
performing this ritual on the dark moon and re-
evaluating at the next dark moon's cycle. This
moon phase is the time of change and rebirth, best
for hexes on contingency.

To give this spell some extra flavor, try stuffing the
mouth with chili powder or cayenne pepper. The
heat is symbolic of burning. Think like a hot foot
spell, but instead their mouth is numb and burning
whenever they have a chain of word vomit.
Along with crossing comes uncrossing. This can get
tricky and requires a lot of materials and energy.
The easiest way to uncross is to gather the
ingredients of the original spell. You don't have to
do all that. Instead, let's learn how to recycle that
energy and transform it into something else. You
don't have to throw it back at the person you think
cursed you. Don't waste your time on that. Instead,

leech that energy they so generously gave you. Nothing would piss off a witch more than that. You are going to take their energy they put into cursing you and benefit from it.

Before we get into the recycling spell, you'll need to know how to make a few other things first. First, we need to make goofer dust. If you don't have access to any of the more exotic ingredients, a 50/50 mix of salt and pepper will suffice.

Goofer Dust

Ingredients:
1 part salt
1 part pepper
2 parts graveyard dirt
1 part ground snakeskin or bone

Where does one get graveyard dirt, you ask? From a grave. You were hoping I wouldn't say that, huh? No folks, this isn't something you want to buy off of Amazon. You need to kindle a relationship with someone that's dead. Yep. You can't just walk up to someone's grave and rob them of their energy. You have to clean the grave. Talk to them. Ask permission.

And don't assume a family member is entitled to give you their energy after death. That's just rude. And if the only time you go to visit Grandpa is to steal his dirt, I don't think he's going to be so happy. He may not break open the coffin, bust the dirt up, and scream "NO." But you will definitely get a vibe from the energy. The dead have less common ways of communication. Be patient and willing to listen.

The next thing we need to know how to make is four thieves vinegar. It got its name because of the four ingredients, as well as an interesting story about grave robbing.

Grave robbers would anoint themselves with this vinegar during the times of the bubonic plague in order to loot corpses that the plague had afflicted and remain healthy.

Our intentions are similar. We are stealing energy that had the intent of a plague and reaping the riches of that energy being recycled and turned into something more pleasant. Simply combine the three herbs below into a bottle and fill the rest of the bottle with the vinegar. Leave out in the sun for three days before use. The herbs used are always debatable, but the common ingredient is vinegar and always only three other herbs.

Four Thieves Vinegar

 Ingredients**:**
Apple cider vinegar
Rosemary
Sage
Mint

Recycling & Uncrossing

Supplies:
Clear quartz
Smokey quartz
Black tourmaline (Or onyx)
Goofer dust
Salt
Four thieves vinegar
Small dish

Instruction:
Take the three crystals and line them up on your altar. To the left, put the tourmaline. In the middle, lay the smokey quartz. And to the right, place the clear quartz.

You are going to create a fuse from the tourmaline, through the smokey quartz, all the way to the clear quartz. Make an even line of goofer dust connecting the tourmaline and the smokey quartz. Then make an even line of salt from the smokey quartz to the clear quartz.

At the end of the line, place the small dish to the right of the clear quartz. Fill it with the four thieves vinegar. After you're all set up, meditate. Hold your palms up, open toward the tourmaline. Focus on all of the anger, hurt, and despair that the hex or shadow has brought on you.

Focus all the energy into your palms, so that it's bursting at your fingertips. Any excess energy, focus on your mind and your gaze. I want you to 'push' with your mind. Imagine a stream of dark clouds pulsing toward the tourmaline. Don't move your gaze or focus until you've let out all the energy you possibly can.

Then, slowly move your palms to the center of the smokey quartz, along the line of goofer. Take your time on this part and imagine the energy surging through the line of dust like a fuse. Like a match on a line of gasoline. As you're shifting your hands, I want you to re-focus. Now that all the junky energy has been expelled from you, start to think positively. Give yourself affirmations. Be nice to yourself. You are molding the energy like clay.

Before you shift over to the clear quartz, start thinking about something specific you want to turn this energy into. Happiness is a good default, or you may wish to be specific about your request. You can turn it into something glamourous, of course! Now, slowly move your palms to follow the trail of salt. Your hands feel less heavy. The energy is flowing more naturally.

By the time you reach the clear quartz, you should feel chills going down your spine. You should be surrounded in feel-good energy.

Now, infuse that into the crystal. When you feel like it's had enough, pick it up gently and soak it in the four thieves. Drown it in the liquid like a baptism. Leave it there for one night, then you may carry it on your person for use. I recommend putting it in a charm bag or gris-gris. After the clear quartz has had a nice bath, clasp the crystal between your palms and say the following chant.

Chant:

"Like sucking the venom
From snake-bit skin
My enemy's energy
Will benefit me

All the hurt, the sad, the pain
Will instead turn into plentiful gain"

If you think you're cursed, you've likely brought it upon yourself. Unless you pissed off another powerful witch, the curse likely manifested over your own guilt and negative energy. As we said earlier, energy cannot be created nor destroyed. Just changed.

So, before you go into an uncrossing and throw it back at someone innocent, it's best to reflect on your own potential guilt and insecurities. Bad luck can be changed. Perspective can be changed. Sometimes, you might end up being your own worst enemy.

Unfortunately, negative energy is harder to change than positive energy. It takes a lot more effort, strength, and willpower. As we know from the law of attraction, birds of a feather flock together.

There are two types of people: those who cheat and those who get cheated on. It's hard to forgive infidelity, but it's not always a deal-breaker in a relationship. Some with the mental fortitude may choose to work on these sexual compulsions with their partner. I don't believe in the 'once a cheater, always a cheater' mentality. I think that if someone truly wants to change, they will.

And as a partner, it's your duty to encourage them to change and support them through mistakes when they are truthful. It won't hurt you any less, but you need to make your partner comfortable being vulnerable. If this is too much for you, do a cord cutting and move on.

Cheaters often respond with fear and defensiveness when being confronted. Be persistent but remain calm when having these difficult conversations. Gaslighting is a defense mechanism that will be a go-to for a cheater. But if you keep your willpower strong and your partner truly does love you, it is possible to have a breakthrough.

Of course, your partner needs to be the one to ultimately change. If being patient and accepting doesn't work or you are just too tired of waiting, you could always use a little glamour magick to speed things up. Dealing with these issues can be draining, especially when you are doing everything right and feel like your partner isn't even trying.

Here is a spell to re-bind your partner to you and 'encourage' them to be faithful.

Anti-Promiscuity

Supplies:
Black person-shaped candle
Red person shaped candle
Hair or any essence from the target
Your blood or any personal essence of choice
3 coffin nails
String
Goofer dust
Dish for burning
Paper or birch bark
Matches
Judgement tarot card

<u>Instruction</u>:

Carve the name of the target on the bottom of the black person candle and your name on the red candle. Set up the two candles side by side in the middle of your workspace. Place a circle of goofer dust around them.

On your paper or bark, write the name of the target. With all your anger and passion, also write down the wrongs they've done. Cross them out and scribble. Be angry when you write. Then, fold the paper and place it in your dish. Along with the paper, add in the essence from both you and the target. In front of the circle, place the Judgement card and invoke Nemesis. (Or any form of Judgement)

JUDGEMENT

Chant:

"Blessed is she, the seer of all
Of wrongs and rights
O' Lady of might

Blessed is she and her sacred law
Advocate of truth
Invoker induce

So, I can see, I take thee into me
By the power of three, so mote it be

Lady Nemesis, I seek thy decree
I seek thy judging degree

Judge where earthly justice fails
Let truth and light now prevail

Let those who break the Lady's law
Face times three of their victim's fall"

After invoking Nemesis, light a match and toss it
into the dish and manifest those bad qualities
burning away. Watch the smoke rise and meditate.
Next, take out your coffin nails. Gently pierce an
eye of the target candle with a coffin nail.

Chant:

"For every woman his eyes gaze upon
That are not mine
Back to me, his eyes are drawn
Or he will become blind"

Next, pierce the heart area of the target candle
with a coffin nail.

Chant:

"For every heart flutter
Stirred from another
May it hurt him three-fold
And his guilt leaves him cold"

Place the last coffin nail into the groin of the target
candle.

Chant:

"He will never be aroused by another

Or so help me, he will smother"

Place the target candle back into the circle and bind the two together with string. Finally, light the two candles.

<u>Chant</u>:

"I shift your sex, your heart, your mind
The love you gave me, only mine
To me and only me, I bind

Unless I will you out of my life
I am yours and you are mine

Your love, libido, belongs to me
Unless love ends, then I set thee free"

From the beginning of time, magick has been used in love spells to bind partners and punish them for promiscuity. What comes to mind is a spell with Hekate referenced in Hekate Liminal Rites by Sorita d'Este. The following passage is from a woman who had been wronged by her man, Delphis, and you can tell by the text how much passion went into this.

"Where are my bay leaves? Bring them, Thestylis! Where are my love charms? Tie a thread of fine crimson wool around the bowl that I may work a spell to bind my lover, who is so cruel to me … But now I bind him with a fire spell. Shine brightly, sweet Moon, I will chant softly to you, Goddess, and to infernal Hekate – before whom dogs shiver when she wanders over the graves of the dead

279

where the dark blood lies. Hail to thee, dreadful
Hekate, and stay with me to the end; make these
drugs as potent as those of Circe and Medea and
golden-haired Perimede.

Draw my lover here, iynx.

First, the barley grains must burn on the fire.
Throw them on Thestylis … Throw them on and
say: 'These are Delphis' bones I throw on.'

Draw my lover here, iynx.

Delphis brought me pain, and so I burn this bay leaf
against Delphis. As it crackles in the flames with a
sharp noise and flares leaving no trace of ash, so
may Delphis' body melt in the flame.

Draw my lover here, iynx.

Now I burn the corn husks. Artemis, you have the
power to move even the steel in Hades or anything
else that is unmovable … Thestylis, the dogs are
howling around town: the Goddess is at the
crossroads. Quick, bang the gong!
Draw my lover here, iynx.

As I melt this wax with Hekate's help, so may
Delphis of Myndus melt immediately from love.
And as this bronze rhombus whirls by the grace of
Aphrodite, so may he whirl at my door.

Draw my lover here, iynx.

Three times I pour libation, mighty goddess, and three times I do say: 'whether it is a woman or a man who lies with him now, may he forget them as quickly as Theseus once in Dea, forgot lovely-haired Adriane.

Draw my lover here, iynx.

Coltsfoot is an Arcadian herb, that makes all the fillies and the swift mares run madly in the hills. May I see Delphis in such a state, coming to my door raving like a madman from the oil of the wrestling school.

Draw my lover here, iynx.

Delphis lost his fringe from his coat: now I shred it and cast it into the ravenous flames...

Draw my lover here, iynx.

I shall crush a lizard tomorrow and bring him an evil drink. Thestylis, take these magic herbs and smear them on his threshold while it is still dark, and spitting say: 'I smear the bones of Delphis.'

Draw my lover here, iynx. ...

Now shall I bind him with my love magic, but if he still causes me pain, he shall beat on the gate of Hades, such evil drugs, I keep for him in my box; Goddess, it is something I learned from an Assyrian stranger." (Theocritus, 270BCE)

In ode to this ancient spell, here is a modernized version to keep a lover faithful and attract him back to you. We'll leave out the death wish, though.

Love Potion #9

<u>Supplies</u>:
Bronze cup/dish
Red twine
Bay leaf
Barley grains
Corn husk
White wine
Dandelion
3 tea light candles

<u>Instruction</u>:
Place your dish in the center of your workspace. Take a long piece of red twine or string and wrap it along the edges of the dish into a spiral. The spiral is reminiscent of Hekate's iynx, shown below. Alternatively, you can do this spell outside and mimic the iynx in chalk and place your bronze dish in the center.

Place a tea light at the top of the circle. One in the southeast of the circle, and one in the southwest. Light the candle on the left. Toss the barley into the dish and chant:

"These barley grains are the bones of my lover. May Hekate's hounds reap them if he intends to cause me pain. Draw my lover here, iynx."

Next, light the candle to the right and take your bay leaf. Toss it into the dish and chant:

"This bay leaf is an offering so that my wish is heard. This plant holds the magick and what makes it work. By offering this bay leaf, see to it he never leaves. Draw my lover here, iynx."

Next, light the top candle and take your corn husk. Add it to the dish and chant:

"I offer this husk to incite trust. May he who drinks this potion feel my each and every emotion. The pain, the hurt, and the worst of the worst. And through love, only then, will lift the curse. Draw my lover here, iynx."

Now, pour the wine generously into the dish. Add the dandelions and let them float on top. Pour the remainder of the wine on the ground on your front porch or in a separate dish for libation and chant:

"I pour libation to the Goddess of the crossroads. May my intent be infused in this fruitful wine. One drink from this and he'll be forever mine. The weeds float to the top and overflow from his cup. For my love is enough. In perfect love and perfect trust.

A drink from this, and my body he cannot resist. A drink from this, and my love will be his only wish. A drink from this, and then sealed with a kiss.

But if that trust is torn apart. If that man destroys my heart. Hekate, meet me at the crossroads. When the moon is dark and the hounds do howl. Befoul that man so none will want him. And so, guilt flows through his every limb. Draw my lover here, iynx."

Leave the dish out overnight. The next day, strain the wine and dispose of the excess ingredients. Serve the wine to your lover to finish the spell and seal it with a kiss. Items used in this spell are not baneful and will not make this person physically ill. The intent of your spell will work as desired. Do not substitute the dandelion for coltsfoot, as in the original spell. The flowers are similar but not safe to ingest. When gathering, be sure to properly identify plant life in your local area.

Recommendations

<u>A Playlist to Make You Feel Witchy AF</u>

Not what you expected in a witchcraft book, eh? Well, how can we talk about glamour and not include the seduction of music? I've curated this list to make you feel like the badass witch you are.

1. W.I.T.C.H. – Devon Cole
2. A Little Wicked – Valerie Broussard
3. No Roots – Alice Merton
4. Dark Horse – Katy Perry
5. The Magic – Lola Blanc
6. Black Magic Woman – Santana
7. Rhiannon – Fleetwood Mac
8. Bad Moon Rising – Creedence Clearwater Revival
9. Goddess – BANKS
10. Superstition – Stevie Wonder
11. Walking On Air – Kerli Koiv
12. Spellbound – Lacuna Coil
13. Howl – Florence and The Machine
14. Save My Soul – Big Bad Voodoo Daddy
15. Witchcraft – Frank Sinatra
16. Dream A Little Dream of Me – Doris Day
17. In The Air Tonight – Phil Collins
18. Mother Earth – Within Temptation
19. Deadly Nightshade – Blackbriar
20. Voodoo – Nyxx
21. The Devil Wears a Suit and Tie – Colter Wall
22. In Hell I'll Be in Good Company – The Dead South
23. Everything Black – Unlike Pluto

24. Blessed Be – Spiritbox
25. As Above, So Below – In This Moment
26. Witch – Apashe
27. Fairytale – IC3PEAK
28. Sink Your Teeth – Eyes Set to Kill
29. We Are the Truth – Mushroomhead
30. Black Sheep – Gin Wigmore

Other Books That Are Worth Your Time

Okay, so aside from the bibliography and texts that I've already referenced, there have been a few books just hit home for me. These titles are unique in their own right.

The one thing I hate about this genre is the oversaturation of beginner's guides. While they are so needed, it's hard to find substance for any intermediate or advanced practitioner. This list is much shorter. Although I've read countless books on the craft, these are the few I feel are truly deserving of a shoutout.

1. Grimoire of the Thorn-Blooded Witch – Raven Grimassi
2. Celtic Lore & Spellcraft of the Dark Goddess: Invoking the Morrigan – Stephanie Woodfield
3. The Witch's Book of Spirits – Devin Hunter
4. Witchcraft Therapy – Mandi Em
5. Treading the Mill – Nigel G. Pearson
6. The Book of Tarot: A Guide for Modern Mystics – Danielle Noel
7. The Encyclopedia of Celtic Wisdom: A Celtic Shaman's Sourcebook – Caitlin Matthews
8. The Magick of Lilith: Calling Upon the Great Goddess of The Left Hand Path – Baal Kadmon
9. Papa Jim Magical Herb Book – Papa Jim
10. The Witches' Book of the Dead – Christian Day
11. Hekate Liminal Rites – Sorita d'Este
12. Utterly Wicked – Dorothy Morrison

Bibliography

Atsma, A. J. (s.d.). *Narcissus (Narkissos)*. Récupéré sur Theoi: https://www.theoi.com/Heros/Narkissos.html#:~:text=NARKISSOS%20(Narcissus)%20was%20a%20youth,his%20arrogance%2C%20spurned%20them%20all.

Coleridge, S. T. (1772-1834). *The Ballad of the Dark Ladié.*

Coué, É. (1922). *Self Mastery Through Conscious Autosuggestion.*

Dennis, T. b. (1910). *Burden of Isis.*

Dessoir, M. (1890). *The Magic Mirror.*

Dutton, D. (2002). *Aesthetic Universals.*

Edie Weinstein, M. L. (2019). The Marilyn Monroe Effect: The Nonverbal Communication of Confidence. *PsychCentral.*

Edie Weinstein, M. L. (2019). The Marilyn Monroe Effect: The Nonverbal Communication of Confidence. *PsychCentral.*

Fresco, G.-R. (s.d.). *Narcissus C1st B.C.* Naples National Archaeological Museum, Pompeii .

Guest, T. b. (1877). *The Mabinogion.* Récupéré sur Sacred Texts: https://www.sacred-texts.com/neu/celt/mab/mab32.htm

Homer, & Evelyn-White, T. b. (s.d.). *Homeric Hymns.*

Jung, C. (1953). *Four Archetypes.*

Leland, C. G. (Original: 1899; Translation: 2010). *Aradia: Gospel of the Witches.*

Nadu, T. (s.d.). *Bhairava 11th Century.*

Orpheus, & Taylor, T. b. (1792). *Hymns of Orpheus.*

Proctor, B. (s.d.).

Rossetti, D. G. (1868). Body's Beauty. *Sinburne's pamphlet review, Notes on the Royal Academy Exhibition.*

Rossetti, D. G. (s.d.). *Lady Lilith.* 1863.

Sappho, & Cox, t. b. (1925). The Poems of Sappho. London.

Theocritus. (270BCE). Idylls 2. Dans t. b. Yardley.

Unknown. (8-10th Century CE). *The Alphabet of Ben Sira.*

Unknown. (s.d.). *Asclepius, Greco-Roman marble statue.* Altes Museum.

Unknown. (s.d.). *From Left to Right: Angels & Demons: Jewish Magic Through the Ages, Keramikos & Bronze Kolossos, Hellenistic, Bronze.* Bible Lands Museum Jerusalem, Musees Royaux d'Art et Histoire, Brussels.

Unknown. (s.d.). *Masterpieces of Ancient Egypt.* British Museum of London, London.

Utamaro, K. (s.d.). *Takarabune.* Yale University Art Gallery, Period: Edo period (1615–1868).

www.ingramcontent.com/pod-product-compliance
Lightning Source LLC
Chambersburg PA
CBHW051135120626
46547CB00012B/816